MINDING OTHER PEOPLE'S BUSINESS

MINDING

OTHER

PEOPLE'S

BUSINESS

WINNING BIG FOR YOUR

CLIENTS AND YOURSELF

DONALD L. DELL

A JOHN BOSWELL ASSOCIATES BOOK

VILLARD BOOKS
NEW YORK 1989

All rights reserved under International and Pan-American Copyright
Conventions. Published in the United States by Villard Books, a
division of Random House, Inc., New York, and simultaneously in
Canada by Random House of Canada Limited, Toronto.

Library of Congress Cataloging-in-Publication Data
Dell, Donald.
  Minding other people's business.
  1. Sports agents—Case studies. 2. Management.
I. Title.
GV734.5.D45 1989 796.068'3 88-27994
ISBN 0-394-57187-8

Manufactured in the United States of America
9 8 7 6 5 4 3 2
First edition

To Carole, my wife, whose love and loyalty have motivated and revitalized me always.

And to Arthur and Stan, wonderful friends and sportsmen, who made it all possible.

Success

"To laugh often and much; to win the respect of intelligent people and the affection of children; to earn the appreciation of honest critics and endure the betrayal of false friends; to appreciate beauty, to find the best in others; to leave the world a bit better, whether by a healthy child, a garden patch, or a redeemed social condition; to know even one life has breathed easier because you have lived. This is to have succeeded."

—Ralph Waldo Emerson

AUTHOR'S NOTE

Even though I am now an international businessman, I continue to see myself in many ways as a tennis player from Bethesda, Maryland. I prefer to consider the enterprise of client management an exciting competition rather than a deadly serious business. Don't get me wrong. Every client is important. Every negotiation is important. But so was every tennis match I ever played.

What I want to say in *Minding Other People's Business* is that any enterprise which primarily involves dealing with other human beings can and should be much more than just a job. A client-oriented business should be just as exciting and just as rewarding as playing at Wimbledon or in the NBA Championship game.

My hope for this book is that it will provide you with some sound principles on the art of dealing with and for clients—practical advice which will have positive applications in your own business. At the same time, I want to give you some special insights into a number of extraordinary people—the magnificent world-class athletes who have been the clients of our firm, ProServ. You will meet Stan Smith, Arthur Ashe, Michael Jordan, Jimmy Connors, Patrick Ewing, Boomer Esiason, Ivan Lendl, Yannick Noah, and many others in settings far removed from those depicted on the sports pages or television screens.

I hope, like most authors, both to inform and entertain. Perhaps I am too ambitious, but I want to do even more. I want to have an impact on the way you work. I want you not only to be more successful, but to enjoy and appreciate that success more fully. In *Minding Other People's Business* I hope to prove the old adage that putting other people first is really the way to come out ahead yourself.

Good luck.

DONALD L. DELL
FEBRUARY 1989
WASHINGTON, D.C.

ACKNOWLEDGMENTS

First and foremost, my sincere thanks and appreciation to John Boswell for his vision, counsel, and judgment on the nature, shape, and content of this book. Without John's friendship, encouragement, efforts, and long hours of work, it would never have been written. As my partner in this book, John was the quarterback and driving force making it all happen.

I would also like to thank Chris Allison and Peter Golenbock, who not only contributed to the writing of this book, but much else about it as well. It was Chris who contributed the original idea for a book on dealing with clients, and Peter made major contributions in organizing the material and searching for a title.

My sincere thanks to Diane Reverand of Villard Books, whose skillful and caring editing helped make this a book of which I am very proud.

I'm sure it is apparent that no single person could build a world-wide organization such as ProServ without the dedication of a lot of talented, committed people. With this in mind, I pay tribute and give thanks to the 150 professional men and women in the ProServ offices around the world who have helped make me look good, and ProServ successful, for so long.

I particularly want to thank my colleagues, David Bagliebter, Pierre Darmon, Dick Dell, Steve Disson, David Falk (who also contributed to the book's content), Sara Fornaciari, Allen Furst, Philippe Pimpaneau, and Jerry Solomon, who, as key executives at ProServ, Inc., give daily leadership to our efforts. The pressures in writing a book of this kind, while maintaining our usual hectic business pace, have placed an extra burden on my personal staff. Yet my Special Assistant, Ivan Blumberg, Administrative Assistant, Karen Sheive Salter, and Executive Secretary, Margaret Van Milder, never missed a beat. They all deserve and have my sincere gratitude.

Finally, I want to give special thanks to my partner and good friend, Robert A. Briner, the President of ProServ Television, Inc., whose encouragement, support, and sharing of these experiences for over twenty years have contributed in spirit and in words to making this book a reality and our professional lives so enjoyable.

CONTENTS

MINDING
OTHER
PEOPLE'S
BUSINESS

BAD SERVICE
IS BAD BUSINESS

Almost overnight, America has shifted from an industrial society to a service economy. This change has created a tidal wave of activity in virtually all client-related fields. According to U. S. Labor Department statistics, there are now nearly forty million entrepreneurs and professionals engaged in service businesses.

Unfortunately, the quality of service has not improved as a result. In fact, service in this country has become so bad that we, as customers and clients, have practically become conditioned to being treated poorly. If we travel by plane and the service is merely bad, our attitude is, "Well, it could have been worse." If we go into a restaurant or department store we almost expect to be abused. There is even a bank commercial on television that states, "We will treat you with the dignity, courtesy, and respect that you deserve." The tag line: "Don't worry. You'll get used to it."

Although the decline of service in this country may be difficult to prove statistically, all you have to do is think back on your own recent personal experiences as a client or a customer, and you probably will come up with all the proof you need.

For instance, walk into an unfamiliar restaurant these days, and the odds of coming out pleased with the service are probably no better than fifty/fifty.

A friend recently told me of ordering a thirty-dollar steak, which came with garden vegetables, in a posh New York restaurant. When my friend asked for french fries instead, he was told, "Sorry, but substitutions aren't allowed. It's our policy."

His dinner partner wanted to complain to the manager, but my friend said to forget it. Any restaurant, he reasoned, that had a "no substitutions" policy with a thirty-dollar entrée hardly cared about customer feedback.

Not too long ago I had a similarly annoying experience. I had just visited a local doctor, which put me in a less than joyous mood anyway. As I was leaving, the receptionist cleared her throat and pointed to a sign on her desk that read, YOU MUST PAY BEFORE YOU LEAVE.

When I explained to her that I didn't have a check with me or enough cash, I was practically restrained from leaving. She treated me as though I was trying to beat the doctor out of his fee.

In both cases, I can't help thinking that these are businesses that survive and prosper on repeat clientele and word-of-mouth referrals. Yet both had instituted service policies that not only discouraged repeat business but made you want to go out and tell the world not to patronize these places.

The point is that it is just as easy, or perhaps even easier, to have the customer or client or patient leave with just the opposite reaction—*wanting* to go out and refer business.

My dentist, for instance, in lieu of a pay-before-you-leave notice, has a little sign up that proclaims, WE SPECIALIZE IN PAINLESS DENTISTRY. Whether it is true or not, you have to appreciate the gesture (even if it's still a dentist's office!). Regrettably, this sort of enlightened approach to service seems to be rare these days, and it is hardly a problem restricted to doctors' offices and restaurants. Rudeness, insensitivity, and thoughtlessness occur at the highest echelons of the business world. Who in business hasn't been mystified at one time or another by a gratuitous comment, unthinking remark, or off-putting behavior like unreturned phone calls from someone who would benefit from behaving with more care?

I have been in the personal service business for many years now, and whenever I hear of a situation where rude, crude, or insensitive behavior has blown a relationship or cost someone a client, it not only offends my professional pride and sense of propriety, but my common sense as well. Any way you slice it, *bad service is bad business.*

To succeed in any client service business you have to succeed on two fronts. First, you have to be good at what you do, an *expert* at the service you are providing. Second, a client must feel comfortable and cared for, satisfied that the service that has been provided is *indispensable*.

As simple and obvious as that may sound, doing the job for clients and also keeping them happy at the same time is one of business's and maybe even life's toughest challenges. As a friend once said, "The only difference between a client and a customer is that the client isn't always right."

How *do* you deal with clients? How *do* you gain the client's respect and maybe even his or her loyalty? How *do* you handle the countless complications that come up? For that matter, how do you attract clients in the first place?

Regrettably, you can't attend a course or go to the library to find out. Although hundreds of books and millions of words have been written on management style, management excellence, and the manager-employee relationship, almost nothing has been written on the most intriguing and demanding of all business relationships: the relationship between clients and the people who represent them.

Yet it is precisely the quality of the client-representative relationship that so often determines the difference between success and failure in business. In this respect, the part-time interior decorator from Paducah, Kentucky, the Washington, D.C., caterer, the Hollywood agent, and the New York ad exec have similar goals and concerns. Each in his or her own way must learn how to get clients, how to keep them, how to keep them at bay when necessary, and how to cope with the daily pressures and emotional strains that representing clients is sure to produce. In this book I intend to address these questions and the skills required in tackling them.

The client relationship at its best is a full business partnership in every sense of the word. I hope this book, by underscoring the difficulties inherent in the relationship, will benefit not only those who have clients, but also the clients themselves.

My real aim is much more ambitious: I want to convince anyone who deals with customers or clients that clients can be the boon, rather than the bane of their existence. To be sure, clients will present you with your greatest "challenges," and also with your greatest rewards. Once you can appreciate and understand the very simple fact that clients, although sometimes a pain, can also be your greatest source of pleasure, you are on your way to transforming what you do for a living into something far more personally satisfying than a mere job could ever be.

I have been a tennis player most of my life, even having achieved some recognition within the sport. I was an all American at Yale, later the number-four ranked player in the United States, and captain of our Davis Cup team. Although winning has always been important to me, the real lesson I learned from tennis is that it is even more important to be a "player"—to be out there in the arena giving it your best shot.

Perhaps if I had been a boxer I would feel quite differently about it. In boxing, losing can be soul destroying, and if you get knocked out badly you may not get up again. With tennis the whole ethic is different: You always live to play another match. If you lose, you still go to the net, shake hands, say, "Well done . . ." and then go at 'em again the next time. What is important is to be competing over and over again. I have always tried to maintain this ethic in my business life—competing for clients and on their behalf.

After attending law school, I went to work for Bobby Kennedy. I've retained a strong sense of idealism from my days with Bobby. One of his favorite campaign slogans was, "Some men see things as they are and say, 'Why?' I dream things that never were and say, 'Why not?' " I took that to heart. Maybe I can't change the world, but I can make a difference in the lives of the clients I represent.

When labor leader Samuel Gompers was once asked what the unions really wanted, his one-word answer was "More." If Bobby Kennedy had ever been asked what kind of place he really wanted America to be, his one-word answer would have been "Better." That was the Kennedy idealism, always striving to make things better.

You might ask, what is so idealistic about making an outrageously wealthy athlete another million dollars a year? It's the great satisfaction I get from doing the best possible job I can do—and being able to share that satisfaction with someone else. If I can represent a kid who has had nothing, and manage him so he doesn't have to worry about financial matters, not only while he is playing, but for the rest of his life, I have accomplished something that makes me feel terrific.

Almost everything else I have learned about providing personal services I have learned from the clients themselves—particularly when the relationship with a client has transcended the boundaries of everyday business into something much more lasting and mean-ingful.

Indeed, my first two clients were Arthur Ashe and Stan Smith, the top two tennis players in the United States when I first started out. Today, they remain two of my dearest and closest friends. One of my favorite stories about Arthur will give you an idea of the feelings we have for one another.

For years, I had pushed Arthur to work on his second serve. After the birth of my twin daughters, Alexandra and Kristina, in 1972, I teased Arthur that if he didn't start improving his serve pretty soon, he was going to deprive my girls of a college education. It became a standing joke between us. During the 1975 Wimbledon tourna-ment, Arthur, who was past his prime by this time, had survived the early rounds on sheer grit and experience. He reached the finals as a 16–1 underdog against Jimmy Connors. No one gave him much of a chance, but just his getting there had been a moral victory.

What people remember about this match, aside from the tennis itself, was Arthur's "meditation" routine during the changeovers. He would close his eyes and seemingly go into a trance. Then he would go out and battle with Connors for a couple of games and repeat the routine again on the next changeover. Arthur's upset win was one of the finest moments of his career. The way he had achieved the victory brought tears to the eyes of most of the fifteen thousand spectators, myself included.

Back home a few days later, I was going through the mail when I came across a postcard that Arthur had sent to Alexandra, his goddaughter. There's a post office truck outside the men's locker room at Wimbledon. Judging from the dateline on the postmark, I could see that writing the postcard must have been one of the very first things Arthur did after experiencing the ultimate moment of his career—winning Wimbledon. Though it was addressed to my daugh-ter, it must have been intended for my eyes as well because this is what he wrote:

Dear Alexandra,
Don't worry kid. You'll get to college now.
                                        Love, Arthur

Much of this book will focus on the more practical aspects of dealing with clients, from getting them to getting the job done for them and even becoming successful in the process.

But to me, that postcard will always be symbolic of the potential the relationship with clients and customers holds for anyone in the business of providing services. Because Arthur, more than being a client and a "business asset," is the greatest of all personal assets—a lifelong friend.

CHAPTER ONE

DO YOU HAVE
WHAT IT TAKES?

When I founded our company, ProServ, Inc., almost twenty years ago by agreeing to represent our first two clients, Arthur Ashe and Stan Smith, I had no idea that it would one day grow into a multimillion-dollar business. Looking back, I can honestly say that representing clients has given me more personal satisfaction than probably anything else I could have done with my life.

After many years of dealing with some of the most gifted and unique athletes imaginable, I have learned—often the hard way—that success in any personal service field requires a good number of distinct, concrete skills in dealing with clients. I have tried to pass on these skills to our client managers to help them avoid some of the pitfalls that, at various times, have entrapped me. It is these skills learned through trial and error that I plan to share with you.

The First Rule of Client Management:
Don't Manage the Client

Whether you are a lawyer, an ad exec, a stockbroker, a banker, a salesperson, or, like me, a manager of professional athletes, the one thing that all clients seem to have in common is that, for the most part, they will respond in kind to the *way they are treated*. If you treat clients fairly and with respect, they will respond in kind. If you treat them with arrogance or indifference, they will treat you with anger. This is hardly a fresh insight. A version of this thinking, in fact, is called the Golden Rule.

Yet the mistake I see over and over again from people just starting out in business is that they assume, perhaps unconsciously, that clients are supposed to behave a certain way. For instance, if they give advice, they expect the client to accept it.

I have learned the hard way that as soon as you expect a client to respond in a certain way, you are setting yourself up for disappointment.

The success of the client relationship will depend less on how the client behaves than on how you handle that behavior. And this brings me to what I believe may be the cardinal rule of client management: *Don't try to manage the client: Manage the relationship.*

Winning Through Accommodation

During my career, I have been very lucky to represent some wonderful clients, many of whom have become my closest friends. But clients can also be difficult. They can be demanding, moody, unreasonable, immature, and irresponsible. Sometimes they can even be just plain unhappy or unpleasant people. There is very little you can do about their persistent shortcomings or basic nature.

What you can control are *your* actions. You have it within your power to control the way you relate to your client, which, in fact, will shape the relationship itself.

If a client acts a certain way, your response will determine whether or not it becomes an unpleasant situation. It doesn't matter what the client says; what matters is what you say and how you handle it. You win clients over, not through intimidation, but through accommodation.

Like it or not, it is your responsibility to accommodate the client, not the other way around. By accommodation, I don't mean automatically acquiescing to the client's demands. What I do mean is knowing when to persist and when to desist, when to press your case and when to back off—knowing, in a nutshell, what button to push, *when,* and how *hard.*

Clients are not always ready to take your advice. Even though advice is, in a large measure, what they are paying you for, they sometimes think they know more than you do. The question is how hard to press and when to back off.

My stockbroker has given me some valuable insights into handling this kind of situation. When he is certain about his advice to a client, he makes sure the client is aware of the confidence he has in the recommendation. He will say something like, "I strongly advise against your making this investment. You should sit this one out." If a client persists in going forward with the buy, the broker attaches a note to the confirmation order saying, "As you can see, we executed your order, but I cannot help wishing you had taken my advice and passed on this one."

If the inevitable happens and the stock loses money, the broker's opinion is on the record about his prior advice. The message he has conveyed says, "I am sorry this was a bad one, but maybe this will help us work together more productively in the future."

The keys are to make sure your clients know how strongly you feel about a particular piece of advice. But, if after you have made your casc as cogently as you know how and they still reject your advice, it is time to back off and let them do it their way. In a casual, but tangible way, you should be sure there is a record of your objection to their actions. When the results are negative, you should try to make the experience one which brings you closer to your clients and enhances their confidence in your future advice.

If your client is pushing to do something either illegal or unethical, you never back off. In these kinds of situations, there can be no compromise.

Tuning In: The Role of Sensitivity

The catch is that you will never know what button to push unless you are first tuned in to clients—sensitized to their moods and needs—and therein lies the art of client management.

One cannot overemphasize this role of sensitivity in dealing with clients—using all of one's senses to pick up even the most subtle signals. It's no coincidence, I believe, that most people who excel in dealing with clients, in any field, happen to be excellent listeners. They are tuned in, not only to what the client is saying, but to what he is not saying as well—what messages are being given, so to speak, between the lines.

You have to be aware if a client all of a sudden becomes testy for no apparent reason, or a little bit more demanding, or is breaking out of his or her normal pattern of behavior. Then you have to look for the reason behind it.

In dealing with athletes, we have a litany of questions we run through. How is the client doing in his or her career? What is the client's relationship with his or her spouse? What in the client's life is not going well? Is the athlete having difficulty with part of his or her game, or have a nagging injury?

Torn ligaments may not affect your particular clients' lives, but think of the factors that do. Is your client facing retirement? Is the company facing new competitive pressures? How *are* things at home?

Many factors come into play, but if there's a problem, it is your job as the client manager to discover what it is, and do something about it. In order to do this you have to be attuned to your client's moods and needs.

Recently, for instance, during a Washington, D.C., tennis tournament, Jimmy Connors was staying at my house with his wife, Patty, and his children. The Sunday afternoon after the tournament was over, several people from the office came out to the house to meet with Jimmy to discuss his schedule over the next six months.

Fortunately, I had only an indirect role in the meeting and was able to judge the climate in the room. I could sense that Jimmy was feeling very uncomfortable almost from the start. I knew he was feeling ill at ease because no one was asking him what he thought or what he wanted. Everyone was trying to get a piece of his time for this appearance or for that exhibition without taking his feelings into consideration, and Jimmy is very sensitive to this kind of treatment.

I had to leave before the meeting was over, but when I came back that evening, the first thing I did was talk to Jimmy privately, and during the conversation I told him, "I want you to forget everything that happened today."

I found out soon that Jimmy was extremely relieved. "I'm glad you said that," he responded, "because that meeting today really upset me. I'm glad someone understands that I have some say in these matters."

Once Jimmy had relaxed, we continued to discuss his schedule. He was so receptive (and relieved) that he agreed to most of what my associates had wanted him to do in the first place—without feeling we were forcing him to do something against his wishes.

By the same token, when you are truly tuned in to your client, you sometimes realize that you can accomplish the most by not necessarily conducting any of the business at hand.

Not too long ago I flew up to New York to meet with our mercurial tennis client, Yannick Noah. I'm not Yannick's direct account executive, but we have been close friends for over a dozen years now. His client manager sensed that Noah had been feeling "down," and since there were several important things we needed to finalize, he felt my presence would be helpful.

During our scheduled two-hour dinner meeting at Kennedy Airport, there were four key items of business we needed to go over with Noah. But when we sat down, he started bringing up his muscle injury and his pending divorce. He was getting depressed just talking about it. I wanted to shift the conversation quickly from stressful topics to more pleasant, relaxing ones. I decided to throw away our business agenda and just be social and try to have some laughs, all based on what I sensed Noah was feeling.

Toward the end of the meeting I said, "Yannick, we came here to talk business, but that's not what's important. What is important is that you always remember that we care about you."

We shook hands and flew our separate ways, he to Brazil and I back to Washington. Though we have never mentioned that meeting again, I feel that I accomplished more for our long-term business relationship that day by simply not doing any business at all.

Take an Aptitude Test

Can anyone, then, be an effective client manager simply by tuning in to one's clients and knowing what buttons to push? In the broadest sense, I think so. But that assertion takes in an awful lot of territory—almost like saying that anyone can play the piano like Van Cliburn and that it's just a matter of knowing which keys to press.

In fact, that Van Cliburn analogy is significant in a number of ways. Like a master concert pianist, master client managers can never spend too much time honing their people skills and fine-tuning their sensitivity to the moods and needs of their clients. Like a talented musician, the people who are best at recruiting and steering their clients in the correct direction probably do have a certain predisposition for client-related businesses—an "aptitude" for it.

Over the years, I have observed a number of personal traits, attributes, and qualities that probably would add up to the perfect aptitude for any personal service or representation business. Obviously, no one possesses all of these qualities, and to a certain degree, you will always be stronger in some areas than others. So, if you want to be successful minding other people's business, you will have to foster these qualities yourself: honesty and integrity, empathy, courtesy, passion, a thick skin, and a sense of fun.

I will refer to these attributes over and over again throughout this book. Together they form the foundation for a healthy give and take between clients and their service providers, whether you are a lawyer, accountant, broker, banker, or contractor.

Obviously, you can't change your basic personality. Through knowing your strong and weak points, you can adjust your behavior accordingly to achieve your goals for the client and effectively manage the relationship.

Furthermore, by being aware of the basic attitudes that make a client manager effective, you can concentrate on improving those areas where you are weak. Behaviors can be learned, and, with a little practice, can be reinforced until they become part of you.

Honesty and Integrity

It should go without saying that if you aren't honest and aboveboard with your clients, you aren't going to keep them for very long. In my business of representing professional athletes, hardly a month goes by that some sports agent isn't accused of paying off a coach, or a relative, or even cheating the clients they represent.

At ProServ we have an overriding philosophy that governs everything we do and can be summed up in two words: honesty and integrity. Is this because we are such terrific, ethical people? Actually, I'd like to think so. My own values are grounded in traditional morality. Since we've been in business, I can't recall hiring anyone who I thought didn't share basically those same values. More to the point, honesty is also good business. In client management, it is vital and essential.

Most companies involving client representation derive much of their business from word of mouth. Whether you are a doctor, lawyer, restaurateur, CPA, or used car dealer, a significant percentage of your business is gained from one satisfied customer telling another. In addition to competence, being known for honesty and integrity is how you build a reputation. These qualities go a long way in gaining the trust and respect of your clients.

When we recruit a player, often we approach the coach initially and ask the coach to set up an appointment. If we approach the player directly, we explain, "We really want to represent you when you graduate from college, but we're not going to call you during your senior year. All we ask is that you don't sign with anybody else until the season is over. How about giving your coach a call and checking us out?" That usually tells the player we have nothing to hide. All we want is a fair, equal opportunity at the end of the season.

The only way we want to operate is aboveboard, walking through the front door. ProServ approaches coaches who we perceive operate on the same basis, and who exhibit a serious concern for the welfare of their players *after* their college careers end. We try to convince coaches that if they will arrange an appointment for us with a particular player on their team and allow us the opportunity to make a presentation with the coach present, ProServ, in turn, will assure the coach that the player will obtain competent, professional, and ethical representation. We have a twenty-year track record to support our claims.

As a result of involving the coaches directly, we have developed good relationships with a number of major college basketball coaches and their programs. Perhaps our closest and longest relationships are with Coaches Dean Smith of the University of North Carolina, John Thompson of Georgetown University, Terry Holland of the University of Virginia, and Ted Owens and his successor Larry Brown of Kansas University.

We take every step to make certain that there is never a hint of impropriety. When basketball superstar Moses Malone graduated from St. Petersburg High School in Virginia, he received an offer to turn pro from the Utah Stars of the old ABA. Moses had signed a letter of intent to go to Maryland, and Maryland coach Lefty Driesell called me. He asked me to evaluate the Stars offer and to advise Moses not to turn pro but to go to Maryland instead.

Ultimately, Moses decided he wanted to turn pro—the first player ever to go directly from high school—and wanted me to negotiate his contract for him. We got Moses a five-year guaranteed contract at $300,000 a year.

You know what we charged Malone for our services? Nothing. It's the only time we've done that. We did it because I didn't want anyone, not Lefty, not a University of Maryland alumnus, not the NCAA, ever to whisper a suspicion that I had tried to steal a high school player for the pros for personal financial gain.

When I'm recruiting college seniors, I run into basketball players who will say, "What's in it for me, man?" meaning, "What are you going to give me up front for the right to represent me?" Or they say, "How are you going to take care of my dad?" My answer is, *"You* take care of your dad."

Whenever we hear that sort of request, we quickly walk the other way. We're not paying off anybody. We play by all the rules because if ever we don't, our reputation is compromised. Once that happens, we're on our way out of business. The fact that all the years we've been in business we've never broken any of the rules helps us, because we can look any parent or coach in the eye and say, "We are reputable people and you can verify it." It's a claim that anyone who deals with clients—from Wall Street traders to the White House's PR staff—*better* be able to make.

In addition to setting uncompromising ethical standards for ourselves, we also demand high standards from our clients. If I find out a client is behaving in a manner antithetical to his or her own best interests, if the client is on drugs and I know it, for example, I tell him or her that we'll help in the withdrawal process, but to continue with us, the client must eventually straighten out.

Greed—like drugs—can also ultimately bring on bad and unacceptable behavior. Although we have negotiated playing contracts for perhaps five hundred athletes, only twice have we had situations where we negotiated lucrative long-term contracts for players, just to have them come back the next year and demand that we renegotiate. Both times we refused and lost the client.

Several years ago we negotiated a contract for pro basketball star Maurice Lucas, in which we doubled his salary and obtained a five-year extension over his old contract. That year, his team, the Portland Trail Blazers, won the NBA championship, so he received even more money in playoff bonuses.

Between seasons Portland center Bill Walton broke his foot, and Lucas was asked to move over to the center position. I got a call from Maurice. "Can you come out to Portland?" he asked. "I want to renegotiate my contract."

I said, "Maurice, we just signed a new five-year contract a year ago. What are you talking about?" He said, "Just come on out here.

They're going to make me a center, and if I have to play center, I want more money."

He had a point. Things change, and something we always try to factor into a player's contract is his relative value to his particular team, but as I flew to Portland to meet Maurice, I suspected there was more going on than met the eye.

When Maurice picked me up, he said, "My phones are tapped. I know they're bugging me. I don't want to talk in my house. Let's go out for a drive."

We drove to a little park on a beautiful day in August and sat on a park bench. I said, "What is this really about?" He answered, "What it's all about is money. I want a new contract or I'm not playing in the middle for them."

I leaned over to Maurice, who is six feet nine, 240 pounds, and I said, "Tell me something. How much is enough? The truth of the matter is, it's never enough, is it? If I got you five hundred thousand dollars you'd want seven hundred thousand. If I got you that, you'd want a million. With you it's never going to be enough, is it, Maurice?"

He looked at me and said, "You're damn right. It's never enough. I'm going to get every dime I can, and I don't care if I have to renegotiate every year."

I said, "Maurice, good luck to you, because I'm not going to be the agent negotiating it. See you around." And I got up and left.

Recently, Lionel Hollins, Lucas's former all-pro guard and teammate at Portland, was quoted by Reuters as saying, "With Maurice, pro basketball was always a contact sport, all *con* and no *tact.*"

There are times when some clients don't want to hold up their end of the contract and make personal appearances. They just don't feel like making the effort. Many times, we insist that they go. We say, "You've signed a contract. They pay you a lot of money. You must go." Usually the client listens.

In the end our role is to take positions which are in the best interest of the client. Part of that role is to make a client do what is right and ethical because we are not just representing the client, we are also representing the client's best interest.

It is your own sense of personal ethics that gives you the confidence you need to tell a client when he or she is out of line.

If a client asks you to do something that is inappropriate or even a little shady—a situation that occurs time and time again in the legal and financial professions—you need to say, "I'm sorry. I don't do that sort of thing." And believe me, instead of being angry, the client will only respect you more for it. The client is paying you for your knowledge and expertise. He or she relies on you to provide your opinion, which is what you should do. By consistently acting ethically and thus in your client's long-term best interests, you will derive pleasure from your work and maintain pride in yourself.

Turning Negatives into Positives

There have been times when we have made mistakes that actually hurt our clients. When this happens you have two choices. One, you can try to cover it up. That never works. Clients usually find out anyway, and when they do, you are embarrassed, your credibility is shot, and ultimately you may lose them as clients.

The only real alternative is to tell clients—honestly and immediately. You can couch the mistakes in the best possible terms, but you have to own up to it. Generally, the clients' appreciation of your being square with them will more than outweigh their irritation over the screwup.

One of our associates once forgot to enter tennis player Chip Hooper in an event. We then tried but failed to get him a "wild card" spot in the tournament. We called Chip and said, "We're sorry, but we screwed up."

Once we talked tennis player Tim Wilkison into skipping an event because we felt he was playing too often. But then we forgot to withdraw him from the tournament on time, and it cost him a $1,600 fine. It was our fault, so we reimbursed him the money and smoothed the whole thing over with the tournament officials.

In both cases our forthrightness actually helped us solidify our relationship with these clients.

The Client Comes First

Finally, in matters of integrity, nothing infuriates me more than seeing a representative put his or her needs before the client's.

I once heard a story about a famous athlete (I won't identify him or his manager here) who signed a licensing deal to wear a company logo as part of his uniform. He got paid $20,000 to wear the logo for one year. The player had a great year, and the next year during negotiations the agent first quoted a $40,000 price but later said it was $100,000.

The company executives were confused. "Which is it?" they asked. The agent said, "Let me explain the confusion. You guys don't know how to utilize my client correctly. So, the total deal comes to a hundred thousand dollars because my client gets forty thousand, and I get sixty thousand as a consulting fee in order to show you how to properly utilize him."

The company executives looked at each other quizzically and said, "Thanks for explaining it to us," and they walked out and canceled the deal. The client was out $40,000 because of the unethical behavior of his representative.

This sort of nonsense, of course, is not unique to the sports business. Product liability lawyers are notorious for "creative compensation" in which they generally fare better than their clients. In business partnerships, general partners often attach special fees for their "services," and end up making excessive profits from their own partners. When this kind of greed goes unchecked, an entire profession can take the heat. The only way you can fight that is to keep your own hands clean.

Jimmy Connors is now a client and a close friend. But in 1974 he sued me, Jack Kramer, and the Association of Tennis Professionals (ATP) for $40 million. It was a political lawsuit. I was general counsel for the ATP, which we had helped establish in 1972, and Connors, a nonmember, was suing the organization and its officers over rules he believed were antitrust violations.

Connors and I ultimately agreed to settle the case among all parties. The terms we agreed to were that Connors would get an insurance policy, and both parties would sign a no-fault agreement. No money was to change hands in the settlement.

After we agreed to the deal, I got a call from Connors's lawyer, whom I knew quite well. He informed me that the deal was off.

"I won't settle the lawsuit on these terms," he said. "I don't care what you and Jimmy agreed to. I spent a year of my life on this case, I'm on a contingency fee, and there's no cash in this deal. Unless you pony up some money for me, I'm not settling this case."

I had known this lawyer for fifteen years, and he is very well respected. But I replied, "That's the most unethical statement I've ever heard a lawyer make. Your job is to settle this case in the best interests of your client, regardless of whether or not you get paid your fee."

The lawsuit was ultimately settled on the original terms.

Along the same lines a writer friend recently told me of submitting a screenplay through his Hollywood agent to the major studios. Several weeks after this process had begun, he received a call from one of his friends at a studio.

"Are you aware," his friend asked, "that your agent is claiming to be your producer and is approaching the studios looking for a coproduction deal?"

When my friend confronted his agent, the agent hemmed and hawed a bit but ultimately admitted that it was true. My friend fired him on the spot.

"I have this silly rule," he told his agent, "that anyone representing me should not make more money off my work than I do."

Empathy

It is hard for me to imagine able representation of clients without some feeling of empathy—a willingness to place yourself in the client's shoes and see the world from his or her vantage point. Fortunately, since most of us at one time or another have also been clients or customers or patients, it is fairly easy to conjure up what a client might be feeling in any given situation. It is also worth remembering the feelings of inadequacy that can arise when you are on the receiving end of advice, rather than the giving end.

When a client hires a representative, it's because he or she has more knowledge in a particular field, whether it's the law, examining your eyes, negotiating a contract, or representing business interests. Although knowledge is power for the representative, that same knowledge can be intimidating for the client. Just the knowledge gap alone can make the client feel insecure and defensive.

If you are not sensitive to this and you consistently make clients feel ignorant or inadequate—and this is much easier to do than you might imagine—then, no matter how pleased they may be with the job you are doing, they already have one foot out the door. As a very successful entrepreneur in his field once said to me, "My ego doesn't demand a fleet of limos or a corporate jet. But ever since I made it, the one perc I've awarded myself is that I will no longer deal with people who make me feel bad."

The best protection against making clients "feel bad" is empathy.

Like the actor who conjures up past personal experiences in order to emote on the stage, I sometimes find it helpful to recall times when someone has made me feel less than terrific, intentionally or otherwise. It invariably helps me be more sensitive to the needs and feelings of the person with whom I am dealing.

I can still vividly recall an incident that happened to me twenty years ago. It was 1968, and I was working in the Lyndon Johnson administration as Sargent Shriver's special assistant at the Office of Economic Opportunity.

OEO was a very controversial program because many thought that Johnson and the Democrats were staffing it with Democrats through the local Community Action Programs around the country—building a political network. The Republicans mistakenly feared that the Democrats were using government funds to build a Democratic organization nationwide.

There was a bill before Congress for further funding for OEO, and Sargent Shriver asked me to go see Republican Congressman Donald Rumsfeld and lobby on behalf of OEO. Rumsfeld was crucial because he had a major influence over his colleagues. Shriver figured that if we could get Rumsfeld to go with us, twenty votes would follow.

Sarge also figured that I would be the perfect person to visit him. I had been an all-American tennis player at Yale; Rumsfeld had been an all-American wrestler at Princeton. A good friend of mine, Pablo Eisenberg, had been Rumsfeld's college roommate.

"I can introduce you to Rumsfeld on a favorable basis," my friend said. "Go see him."

I set up an appointment and went down to Rumsfeld's office. Three minutes into my presentation, he said, "I'm not going to vote for more funding for that damn OEO program." I gave him all my arguments, and then he got angry. He said, "I know what you're doing here. Shriver sends a jock down here. You think I'm a jock because of my background. You went to Yale. I went to Princeton. I was an all American in wrestling. So he sends a jock down here to lobby me."

With that, he got up and stormed around his desk. He's short and powerful, and as he barreled toward me, he said, "Goddamn it, get out of my office. I don't want to hear any more about this OEO nonsense."

I actually thought he was going to throw me out physically. As he neared and then passed me, I realized he was merely reaching to open his door. "Get out," he ordered, "and tell Shriver not to send any more of you PR jock types down here."

It was one time in my life when I can remember feeling totally humiliated, and now—whenever I have a "bad attitude" about a client—I often use that memory to keep my own behavior in line with what I truly believe makes for good business: the Golden Rule.

The next time a client complains about feeling ignored or insignificant or not being far enough up on your priority list, if you can feel a little empathy for the person, you are far more likely to come back with the appropriate response.

Courtesy

Even the words *politeness* and *courtesy* tend to make our eyes glaze over. But in the service business, the two go hand in hand with success. The need to be treated politely and courteously may be of more consequence than people realize. Most of us, I believe, harbor a deep-seated longing to be treated in a humane and courteous manner.

When someone refuses to return our phone calls, or keeps us waiting for a long time, or takes calls during a meeting, or looks impatient or distracted when we speak, we'd like to think we are above caring about that sort of thing. But no one is. When we are treated rudely, we're being told that we don't matter. Conversely, when we are treated with decency and courtesy, we're being told that we matter a lot. What other signal would you ever want to give your clients?

The point is that politeness and courtesy are good business. I recently read a profile of Frank Mancuso, who, after a major shake-up at Paramount Pictures a few years ago, was named its new chairman. Many industry insiders figured he would fall flat on his face, in part because he had the reputation for being a gentleman in a business not known for gentlemanly behavior.

Instead, Paramount became the top-grossing studio for two years in a row (the first time any studio had accomplished that feat in a decade), and much of this success is now being attributed to Mr. Mancuso's polite and courteous style of doing business.

When the producers of the Australian movie *Crocodile Dundee* came to America to seek distribution, they interviewed all the major studios, but finally settled on Paramount. Paul Hogan, the movie's star and one of its producers, said of Frank Mancuso's style, "He was the only one who didn't treat us like a bunch of colonials who had just happened to get lucky."

In this case, politeness and courtesy paid off to the tune of about $150 million.

At ProServ, we try to treat people with courtesy and politeness. We sometimes fall short in this important area, but we are always trying to improve.

Passion

Have you ever had a lawyer tell you why a deal couldn't be done or your accountant tell you why you owe even more money to the government than you thought? The knee-jerk response is usually to think, "These guys aren't doing their jobs."

Regardless of what these representatives are saying, they seem to have failed you. When you hire someone to do a job for you, particularly in areas such as taxes, the law, and personal representation of all sorts, you want more than a representative; you want a fighter, a professional who will take your cause, whatever it might be, and elevate it to the equivalent of a holy war.

I am a lawyer and most of our client managers are lawyers, though given the choice between hiring someone with good legal skills and good people skills, I would always choose the latter. One thing I will say for a legal education is that it does indoctrinate you in the advocacy system: representing your client to the best of your abilities and pulling out all the stops on the client's behalf. It is something which not only the client respects, but also the opposition.

I can't imagine being a good advocate for your client without some degree of passion. Think of two of the most famous speeches— William Jennings Bryan's "Cross of Gold" speech or Clarence Darrow's defense at the Scopes Monkey Trial. The one common denominator is that they were often remembered even more for their passion than their content.

Several years ago Henry Kissinger got in trouble when he admitted to a reporter that sometimes he felt like the marshal of an Old West town, a "lone gun" hired to get the bad guys and keep the world safe for democracy. That isn't necessarily the self-image you want your Secretary of State to have, but I think most Americans secretly loved that image—you knew Kissinger was going to get the job done.

It is passion for your client's cause that empowers you to turn defeats into victories, no's into yesses, and problems into solutions. It is what allows you to be persistent, to persevere, to overcome the odds, and it is what makes you keep "raising the bar" on the client's behalf—getting the client a better deal than even you had thought was possible.

I have a theory that 90 percent of what clients expect from someone representing them is fairly cut-and-dried, whether it is an ad campaign or a catered dinner or a stock transaction. If we are representing a "million-dollar" client, chances are that most of our competition would be able to bring home a deal pretty much in that range.

The great challenge for me is to negotiate more than anybody else could. This is where you find the award-winning ad campaign, the dinner of the season, or the perfectly timed stock sale. And the key is passion—for the client, for his or her case or cause, and, in my case, for the negotiation process itself.

For example, in 1985 Patrick Ewing graduated from Georgetown after leading the Hoyas to the NCAA finals three times in four years, including the National Championship in 1984. Needless to say, recruiting Patrick, the most dominating player in the country, was intense.

On the day Coach Thompson scheduled ProServ to make its presentation, I was in Japan on other business. David Falk, who began his career as my special assistant fourteen years ago, and is now my partner and close friend, was in charge of the presentation as the head of our team sports division. When I received a telex from David in Tokyo several days later informing me that Ewing had selected ProServ to represent him, I was elated for the company and proud that our people had successfully signed the most important player in the United States.

When David and I began planning our strategy for the Ewing negotiations, the market for the number-one pick in the draft had been established by Ralph Sampson and Akeem Olajuwon, the "twin towers," drafted back-to-back by the Houston Rockets in 1983 and 1984. Both received contracts averaging approximately $1.2 million per year. Everyone—including the New York Knicks, who drafted Patrick number one in 1985—expected Ewing to receive a similar contract. Instead, we negotiated the largest deal in the history of team sports, in excess of $30 million over ten years.

Many factors contributed to this result. In my mind, the single biggest factor was our determination to surpass everyone's expectations—including our own—and to break new ground in professional basketball.

We could never have made this deal if we had not been bound and determined to beat our best-case expectations. Passion in any personal service business is partly your ego on the line for someone else. In many ways, the victories that result are personally the most gratifying because they are not private; they can be shared with someone else.

Finally, I don't think I could go as hard or as continually as I do if I didn't have a real passion for my work. I get calls from clients almost every night. I'm in the office all the time. Although I often feel harried, I rarely feel a sense of drudgery about anything I have to do.

How do you go about injecting passion into your work? There are people who can take almost any task and turn it into drudgery, and there are others who can take that same task and turn it into a game or a contest and make it exciting and exhilarating. Your passions are fired just by the realization that you are involved in a positive way in the life of your client.

In any personal service business, much of the passion for what you do has got to come from the most obvious source—all the people with whom you are dealing.

In a polite, indirect way, I once asked the person who cuts my hair how he could come in and do the same task over and over and over again and still get out of bed and go to work each day. He looked at me as if I were crazy and began to tell me about all the fascinating conversations he'd had with customers just that day. "Sometimes," he said, "I can hardly wait for a customer to come back for his next visit, because I want to continue our conversation."

It is the clients I care about who make the job worth doing and life worth living. It is these clients who inject passion into my work and give me a sense of mission, and it is these clients who make me genuinely excited about coming in to work each day.

A Thick Skin

In order to represent clients you need to be sensitively attuned to their needs, treat them with politeness, dignity, and courtesy, always deal with them in a fair and honest manner, and then when they whine and complain and treat you with scorn, just let it roll right off your back. Obviously, if you could attain this level completely, you'd be the picture in the dictionary next to the word *perfection*.

There is no getting around the fact that effectively dealing with clients demands a dual nature: soft on the inside, hard on the outside. A thick skin is probably the toughest thing to develop, but I'd be less than truthful if I pretended it wasn't called for every now and then.

No one should simply allow themselves to be abused. When this becomes a problem I do a quick calculation: How important is the client to me in relation to the grief I am getting? In some cases, you just have to accept the reality that part of what the client assumes he or she is paying for is your tolerance. It comes with the territory.

Thick skin is keeping cool when a client plays the "What have you done for me lately?" tune, or responds after you've spent two months in hard negotiations by saying, "What do you mean, you got me a hundred thousand? I'm worth three times that." A big part of the job is dealing, in effect, with the client's ego, and believe me, all clients have an ego.

When an acquaintance of mine first got into the business of personal representation, a letter from one of his new company's bigger clients was already on his desk awaiting his arrival. It began: "Welcome to the firm. Your first priority is working for me."

His first instinct was to tell off the client, but four years later they were still working together—very profitably. "It became a challenge," he told me. "This person was such a jerk I made a game out of it—seeing if I could anticipate what outrageousness he would come up with next and get ready for it. To this day the client doesn't know what I really think of him."

One of the keys in dealing with obstreperous clients is anticipation, which will be discussed later on under the topic of controlling the client. Over the years, I have also developed certain techniques for dealing with clients who are too whiny or demanding or uncooperative, and I will get to these later on as well. But for now, it's simply worth noting that if you are going to have clients, there will be times when you have to be able to take it.

Even before Patrick Ewing had finished his senior year at Georgetown, various individuals aspiring to represent him began to wage a "reverse recruiting" campaign. The basketball grapevine began to buzz with the prevailing wisdom that "It's probably a waste of time to recruit Ewing because the Georgetown players always sign with ProServ." Since we had not even met Patrick, these "suggestions" not only surprised us, but raised concerns that Patrick might think ProServ had initiated them. We called John Thompson to assure him that ProServ had nothing to do with these rumors and requested that he advise Patrick accordingly. Thompson amazed me with his response: "Grow up." And that was that. Of course, John was absolutely right. There was no room for childish worries over rumors.

A Sense of Fun

Last, and perhaps also most crucial, to be a success in the personal service business, or any business for that matter, you have to have a good time doing it.

I came out of a tennis era where the fun of playing the game was almost as important as whether you won or lost. Back in those days of amateurism, my contemporaries thought they were getting away with murder simply because people were willing to pick up their travel expenses!

Today, of course, the emphasis is on money—money, money, and more money—to the exclusion of anything else. And look what has happened as a result. Bjorn Borg retires at age twenty-six because he can no longer take the pressure; John McEnroe has an emotional outburst on the court every time he goes out; and top female players such as Tracy Austin and Andrea Jaeger quit before they're out of their teens.

Don't get me wrong. I'm as delighted by the growth of tennis as anyone. In fact, I'm usually the first person to be blamed for its commercialization. However, I find it difficult to understand how earning a couple million a year, even when you lose, should make life all that miserable.

It is worth keeping in mind that when a player does win, especially when it's an upset, how many times have you heard, "I just went out there and tried to have some fun?" It has been proven over and over again by both psychologists and world-class athletes that if you can just go out there and have a good time, your performance will improve as well.

The fun of professional tennis, just like the fun of work, should be in the achievement of competing. It is the high you feel when you do your best and the result shows. Nonetheless, you have to balance your life to keep the "game" in your work, whether it's as a professional athlete or as a business person.

I think it's high time for professionals from all walks of life to learn not to take themselves so seriously. Having fun ranges from being able to laugh at your own mistakes to figuring out ways to make your job more interesting and entertaining, from joking with your co-workers to not making a martyr of yourself. It involves factoring in time away from work and making your work as "unworklike" as possible.

I really enjoy many of our clients and try to see them on a social basis as often as I can.

It's also invigorating to be a little kid at times. There is something to be said for cutting up every once in a while, tweaking the nose of authority, or doing something that the "grown-up" in you says you shouldn't be doing. I think "being a kid" plays a far greater role in business success than psychologists now realize.

For instance, you know all those angry letters you are supposed to put in your drawer and save for twenty-four hours because they are probably not in your best interest to send? I'm afraid I've probably sent out more than my share. Although there are times when I've regretted it, the psychic benefits of letting off a little steam counterbalance these indiscretions.

Remember Donald Rumsfeld, who kicked me out of his office for trying to get him to support OEO? The irony of the story is that when Richard Nixon was elected President in 1968, whom did he choose to head OEO but Donald Rumsfeld himself, the very man who told me he would never vote another penny in appropriations for OEO!

On learning that Rumsfeld was appointed, I could not resist writing him the following letter:

> Dear Don,
>   How well I remember when trying to advocate the OEO program, you literally threw me out of your office. I wonder if your viewpoint will change now that you are the OEO's new executive director?

I don't know how he reacted when he got the letter, but it did make me feel good to express myself. Taking actions others may deem "inappropriate" toward people who have made me feel bad is one of the ways I know I can let off some steam. It is the safety valve that keeps me from getting ulcers.

I remember once going to see the chairman of E. F. Hutton. The former president had been George Ball, who had founded the Grand Champions tennis circuit for Hutton. When Ball left E. F. Hutton to become the president of Prudential Bache, he took some key Hutton executives with him. Now I was faced with the task of convincing the current chairman, Robert Foman, to renew sponsorship of the tennis circuit founded by Ball, a man whom he now disliked intensely.

At our meeting the chairman said, "Mr. Dell, the circuit was pretty successful last year, a lot better than we'd anticipated. But we are not going to renew. The problem is you're playing in ten cities, and we have offices in seventy-two cities around the country. It's unfair to the offices that are left out."

"No problem," I immediately countered. "Suppose we rotated the cities, ten new cities this year, a different ten next year?"

"That wouldn't quite work," he said. And every time I made an argument, he'd counter. After some more brief jousting the chairman finally said, "Mr. Dell, we've been talking about six minutes, and you can talk for the rest of the afternoon if you would like. But under no circumstances is E. F. Hutton going to renew this sponsorship."

As I was sitting there, I thought to myself, "This is a lost cause. There are a lot of things I can turn around, but this is not one of them." As I headed toward the door I thought to myself, "What the hell. Why not?"

"Oh, I almost forgot," I said. "George Ball asked me to say hello." At the mere mention of George Ball's name, Foman changed color, and because I had been dreading this meeting I felt more relieved than I had in days.

The role of humor in business, across the board, cannot be underestimated. It serves many functions: It can be used to break the ice, it can diffuse tense situations, it allows you to discuss subjects that might otherwise be uncomfortable to discuss, and it fosters camaraderie. In short, humor is a safety valve, not just in dealing with clients, but in dealing with all aspects of business.

I can remember negotiating an extension of Arthur Ashe's contract with Head for the Arthur Ashe competition racquet. We had settled on a five-year agreement with a minimum guarantee of $500,000 a year, and we were just about finished when Tom York, the president of Head's parent company, AMF, came into the room, ostensibly to give the deal his approval.

Instead, he balked. Even though Arthur's previous royalties had considerably exceeded $500,000 annually, the sheer size of that sum disturbed him. "There is no way we can pay Arthur, or any other tennis player, that kind of money," he said. "Hell, I don't make that kind of money and I'm the president of this company."

There was an awkward moment of silence, and then I said, "But Tom, you don't serve as well as Arthur either. When you win Wimbledon, you'll get half a million dollars, too."

He looked at me and roared with laughter. In the end, we signed the contract.

In any personal service business, the greatest source of pleasure, of course, is the people around you, the people with whom you work, the people you sell to, and mainly the people you serve—the clients. If you think about it, where have you had your best laughs? That should tell you something. I have had a teasing relationship with many clients over the years. I can playfully tease them, and that invariably leads to an affectionate relationship between us. They tease me back. Once I know I have that kind of rapport, I know our relationship can withstand the tough and difficult times. That is the kind of relationship that anyone dealing with clients should be trying to build.

CHAPTER TWO

GETTING
CLIENTS

Even if you are the world's best at what you do, if you aren't very good at selling clients on yourself and your services, you're never going to have much of a business.

In the sports world there appear to be more agents around than players, which isn't any wonder when you consider the hundreds of millions of dollars that are at stake. As most of these representatives quickly learn, who you are, or how much you know, doesn't guarantee you one nickel in income. Indeed this is true of most service businesses, from law firms to ad agencies to brokerage houses to medical groups: Just hanging out a shingle guarantees nothing.

I'm sure this is why the first question I am always asked whenever I speak to law or business groups is: How did I get my first client? The answer is luck, timing, and the good sense to recognize both for what they were.

The Roll of the Dice

The role that luck and timing play in success can be debated end-lessly. For the most part, I believe that you make your own luck. Anyone who claims to be "just plain lucky" is probably being falsely modest. Despite that belief, I can honestly say that had I been born ten years earlier or later, I probably would have ended up in a different profession.

Until 1968, tennis was a sport played mostly by amateurs. A handful of players like Pancho Gonzales, Pancho Segura, and Jack Kramer toured as pros, but like golf of the Bobby Jones era, it was the amateurs who received all the praise and attention.

All that changed when the first United States Tennis Open was held in 1968. It was the first time in America that pros and amateurs competed head to head for prize money. I was captain of the United States Davis Cup team that year, and Arthur Ashe, who was a first lieutenant in the army and a member of our Davis Cup squad, won the 1968 U.S. Open.

After Arthur's win there was tremendous pressure on him to turn pro. The promoter who wanted to sign him was a man named George McCall. McCall offered Arthur a total guarantee of $400,000 for five years. That was a tremendous sum of money in the tennis market back in 1968.

Arthur came to me for advice because I was the Davis Cup cap-tain, I was a lawyer, and I was his friend. He said, "Do you think I should take this offer?" I told him, "Arthur, I'd wait. Your name value is going nowhere but up. You're playing well. You are allowed to win prize money now. You're in the army. You're single. You don't need the contract now. I think the money will be bigger if you wait." So he did.

Meanwhile, for several months I had also tried to play matchmaker between Arthur and Mark McCormack. Mark, who had started with Arnold Palmer, had practically invented the sports marketing business. He had a solid reputation for merchandizing and licensing, which is what Arthur really needed. I knew Arthur had the charisma to become the "Arnold Palmer of tennis," and I figured that Mark would be helpful to him.

One morning after one of our several meetings with McCormack, Arthur and I were in a taxi going down the FDR Drive in New York when Arthur turned to me and said, "How many more times are you going to do this? How many more times are you going to take me to see McCormack?"

"I thought that's what you wanted," I said.

He said, "Why don't you represent me?"

I replied, "I'm not in that field. I'm a lawyer, not an agent. I'm just captaining the Davis Cup for a couple more months, and then I'll go back to my law firm in Washington. Besides," I added, "I never thought about it."

"Why don't you think about it?" Arthur said.

Life is funny that way. If tennis hadn't been just about ready to explode or if I had succeeded in getting Arthur an agent, which I had tried my darndest to do, I'm sure I would be in a different line of work today.

About a week after our conversation, I called Arthur. I said, "It's possible that I may open my own law office. If I do, I'd be very interested in representing you. You would be my first client."

Once I decided to go into the business of representing tennis players and Arthur had agreed to be my first client, I knew immediately who my second client should be—Stan Smith. Stan, with his blond California good looks and big power tennis game, was and is any client manager's dream.

Stan was a key member of the two winning Davis Cup teams I captained, and during the many hours we were together we discussed what open tennis might mean to world-class players and also my desire to stay in the sport in some meaningful way.

When I called Stan to tell him I wanted to fly out to meet him at the Balboa Bay Club near Los Angeles, where he was playing in a small tournament, I was pretty sure he knew the purpose of my visit. He seemed eager to see me.

Stan is so friendly and easy to talk to that there was never any strain involved in asking him to put his career in my hands. After only a few minutes of discussion, we sealed the relationship with a handshake. That relationship is now in its twentieth year.

Is there any lesson to be learned from this? Yes, I think there is a major one. Many business people, at one time or another, are tempted to go out on their own, particularly in service businesses where the start-up costs are often minimal. Once you've developed the necessary skills and expertise, my advice would be to try it, but only when the timing is right. The key is to recognize your Arnold Palmer or Arthur Ashe when he or she comes along, and with a little less persuasion than it took in my case. But timing and luck certainly helped.

Doing Your Homework

Perhaps because my first two clients fell into my lap, I have been extremely conscious of the step-by-step process one must go through in order to recruit a client successfully. As a holdover from my training as a lawyer and litigator, where I saw that most trials were won or lost before anyone entered the courtroom, I can promise you that the first steps must be taken well *before* you meet the client face-to-face.

One cannot overestimate the importance of doing your homework, of knowing everything there is to know about the client *before* you give your presentation. So often it is the mutual acquaintance or reference or little-known fact that can turn the tide. When you've done your homework, the client knows it. At the very least, you send the strong message that you are thorough and professional and that you cared enough to make the effort.

Who Is the Key Advisor?

In our business, and I think this is true of many personal service businesses, there is often a third-party key advisor—a coach, a parent, a spouse, a local team booster—whose influence on the client is so great that it is the advisor even more than the client who must be courted, as he or she often will influence the final decision.

I cannot stress enough the importance of finding this person. In a later chapter, I'll discuss the corporate environment and how to find the most influential persons in that jungle. For smaller businesses and individual clients, it's usually more clear-cut. But the only way to determine who that advisor is and how strong his or her influence is over the prospective client is to take the time to beat the bushes and pound the pavement—doing your homework.

If I had to name the one element common to most of our successful recruitments, it would be learning to identify the key advisor. In most failed recruiting efforts, this element was most notably missing.

I can remember meeting with a tennis player we thought we had successfully recruited. His wife had attended the meeting as well. Although I had made a number of "charming" comments to her throughout, my business remarks had been addressed strictly to the player. If I had been more diligent, I would have known that his wife was a lawyer and handled all his business affairs. This failure, and my inattentiveness to her, cost us a client.

A failure to do our homework—or at least a failure to dig deep enough to draw the right conclusions—also resulted in our losing the

opportunity to represent the college basketball player of the year
several years ago, Ralph Sampson.

Ralph was a high school player from Harrisonburg, Virginia, of
nearly legendary proportions. After a national high school recruiting
battle, Ralph decided to attend the University of Virginia. I had
graduated from Virginia Law School so I already had strong ties to
the school. In fact, Emerson Spies, who taught me property law at
Virginia and later served as dean of the Law School, is currently an
advisor to our financial services division. ProServ had also represented University of Virginia standout Wally Walker, who was
drafted number five in the country in 1976, and thus began a cordial
relationship with Head Coach Terry Holland, who was then in his
first year at Virginia.

At the conclusion of each of Ralph's first three years at Virginia,
Terry invited me down to Charlottesville to advise Ralph on whether
to leave school early for the NBA. In each instance, I counseled him
to stay in school. ProServ's involvement with Wally Walker (and
later with Marc Iavaroni), and my annual trips to Charlottesville,
naturally led to Terry Holland's becoming a good friend.

When David Falk and I were ready to go down to Charlottesville
to make our presentations to Ralph, we asked to go last. Appoint-
ments with representatives had been scheduled all week. Since Coach
Holland had organized the meetings, that's where he put us.

We met with Ralph, Holland, and Ralph's mother, father, and
sister. After we finished our presentation, we were all getting up from
the table, and I asked, "Hey, Ralph, what are you doing tonight?"
Ralph's mother answered, "We're going back to our house to have
dinner."

At that point Terry interrupted, "Mrs. Sampson, why don't you
have Donald and David come back with you, and you can chat over
dinner." She replied that she and Ralph were too tired and—bang!,
just like that, there was something in the way she said it, the way she
finessed it—that told me we were in big trouble.

That evening, I called Holland at home and he said, "Donald, your presentation was outstanding. It was much better than anybody else's: the numbers, the concepts, the marketing plans. Like pros versus amateurs. But I have to tell you, there is this other agent, Tom Collins, and Ralph's mother is crazy about him."

I said, "Coach, what was that business about dinner at the end of the meeting?" He was a little embarrassed. "I hate to tell you this, but when Collins was here yesterday, the mother invited him back to the house for dinner with the family."

I hung up the phone and I said to David Falk, "We blew it. We're going to lose Sampson." It was clear to me that the mother had much more say in Ralph's affairs than we had known—much more say, in fact, than even his basketball coach at Virginia!

Ever since then I've teased Terry, "Well, Coach, that's great. I spend four years of my life making you my best friend at Virginia and then you tell me it's Ralph's mother who calls all the shots!"

But I can't blame anybody but ourselves. Maybe if we had done our homework better—maybe if we had asked all the right questions, or even some of the questions a little earlier, things might have turned out differently.

As a footnote, it's much more effective to make the advisor a partner rather than a competitor. When we recruited the Argentine tennis star Gabriela Sabatini, neither she nor her parents spoke fluent English. We had to rely totally on her coach, Patricio Apey, to act as our go-between. If he had felt uncomfortable with or threatened by us, he could have totally sabotaged our efforts, and we probably would not have signed Gabriela. Fortunately, the coach didn't see us as a threat to his relationship with her. We did everything we could to make him feel like a partner in our efforts. We did whatever was necessary to indicate to him that he was part of our team. He, in turn, saw that our interest in Gabriela was not only different, but compatible and complimentary, and he did what he could to help us with her family.

The same thing applies in our dealings with corporations. Often the company to whom we are selling will have an outside advisor—a consultant, an ad agency, a marketing firm—whose judgment will be sought regarding one of our sports promotions. If we can enlist the aid and support of these outside advisors, not only does it make our sales job a lot easier, it usually greases the wheels for us internally with the corporation.

First Impressions

I am a great believer in the importance of first impressions. Needless to say, a negative first impression will probably be the prospective client's last impression. Favorable first impressions form the point of reference for much of what will come later on in the client relationship. Two and three years after the fact I have had clients recall in vivid detail things that happened or that were said during our initial meeting.

In sports recruiting, in particular, athletes grow wary, sensing that everyone wants a piece of them, and they are sizing you up from the moment you walk through the door. But even if you are representing a harried entrepreneur or a rising corporate star, the response is going to be the same. More than half of a client's overall impression will be formed in the first ten to twenty minutes spent with you.

This is why, first, I want my actions to be natural. If I am meeting a young athlete, how I walk in and greet him or her is very important. I want to give a firm handshake, look the athlete in the eye, smile, and be warm and friendly. I want to be relaxed, but also businesslike. What might be appropriate for one of his or her friends is not appropriate for me. I'm not going to walk into a meeting and give a young athlete a high-five, that's for sure.

I also want my dress to be, above all else, appropriate. The way you dress is rarely a big positive, but it can be an amazing distraction or make a negative impression. The secret is to dress in a professional way.

Obviously, the better you know the people with whom you are meeting the more latitude you have. But if you are meeting someone for the first time, you can never go wrong wearing clothes that show "respect": Whatever the "jacket and tie" is for your profession, wear it for that first encounter. Otherwise, it's just a matter of tailoring your clothes to the occasion.

The Commonsense Part

Much of making a favorable first impression is doing—and avoiding—as common sense would dictate. If I showed up, for instance, at an initial meeting in blue jeans or a warm-up suit, not only might I look foolish, but it wouldn't convey a very good message about my work ethic to the client.

Following are some other commonsense points:

• *If the meeting is at your office, make sure the receptionist and secretary are aware of the prospective client's visit.* A polite, friendly, efficient receptionist can score a lot of points before the game has even started. I know of one company that posts a highly visible "visiting VIPs" board on the wall behind the receptionist. This board lists the names of that day's important visitors. Everyone likes to see him or herself referred to as a VIP.

• *Be on time.* There is a kind of Richter scale for people who are kept waiting in the reception rooms: *2* is twice as bad as *1, 3* is twice as bad as *2,* and so on. As the waiting time increases arithmetically, irritation increases exponentially.

If a small delay is unavoidable, again, the receptionist can be a lifesaver by making the guest feel comfortable. After a wait of five or ten minutes, it helps if the receptionist calls to say, "I just want to remind you that Mr. Jones is still waiting." It may not hurry things along, but it makes the person waiting feel better.

If the wait is any longer than a few minutes, some action is needed. We will often move our guest into a conference room or even a spare office where he or she can make calls and conduct other business.

Punctuality is not one of my strong suits. In fact, it is my worst business trait, so when I'm running behind, I will often have one of my associates begin without me. Even if the substantive part of the meeting has to wait, clients don't mind going through some preliminary matters just so long as they know you are conscious of their arrival and are making the effort to use their time productively.

• *Avoid heavy conversations or controversial subjects.* Why risk saying anything offensive? Once you get to know the client, obviously this becomes less of a worry. The exception is if you know you share a strong point of view on a particular subject with the prospective client. You can make that work to your advantage.

• *Observe unwritten etiquette.* Whether it's lighting up a cigarette or making an off-color remark, why do anything in an initial meeting that the client might remotely find objectionable? Remember, you are actively being judged, so use your common sense and be aware of what you say and do and how it is affecting others in the room.

One time during a meeting with a potential corporate client, I became so engrossed in selling ourselves, I was totally unaware that I had said "Jesus Christ" several times and not once had it been in prayer. After the meeting my associate told me that every time I had said this, one person in the room visibly winced.

We did not get the account.

• *Don't run off at the mouth.* Talk less, listen more, and ask a lot of questions. There's more about this later on. But being a good listener is one of those business "arts" that can't be stressed too often.

• *Don't engage in false flattery.* Flattery will get you somewhere—as long as it's *legitimate.* I'm particularly attuned to this because in any business the prospective clients have heard it all before, and they can smell insincerity a mile away. Bring up the fact that you'd love to represent the prospective client because of his or her real accomplishments, not because the person is both the greatest athlete and the greatest person who ever lived all rolled into one.

• *Speak plainly but don't talk down to the client.* A patronizing know-it-all tone with a client is the kiss of death. You want to speak plainly and simply, but don't sound as though you are trying to simplify the complexity of what you do so that the uninformed (like the client) can understand. The tone you use and the words you choose can undermine almost any other good feelings the client might have for you in a meeting.

• *Don't criticize the competition.* When soliciting clients, even the vaguest expression of a negative feeling about your competition can make you appear to be defensive or insecure. If you can't say something good about your competition, don't say anything at all. Even when we lose a client who has picked someone we respect, we will let the athlete know he or she has made a reasonable choice.

• *Be prepared and be organized.* Come organized—and stay organized. Even the slightest appearance of disorganization speaks volumes to the prospective client about how it will be to work with you later on. Shuffling papers in search of a missing document or rummaging through a briefcase while everyone waits can bring an upbeat, enthusiastic meeting to a screaming halt.

Do your homework and be prepared. Get your act together before the meeting and not during it. If more than one person is making the pitch, make sure you know the roles everyone is going to play. Nothing can turn off a prospective client faster than confusion or obvious lack of preparation.

Nothing, that is, except perhaps mispronouncing the name of the
client. Talk about lack of preparation. I remember a meeting with
a cologne company to discuss promotional opportunities in tennis.
Throughout the meeting I kept saying "and this tournament sponsorship could do a lot for Aramis," only I kept pronouncing it
A-ram'-is, with the accent on the middle syllable instead of on the
first. This was one of those faux pas that was so unpardonable, it was
actually overlooked by everyone else at the meeting.

First, Get Their Attention

Creating a good impression—or avoiding a bad one—gets you in the
game, but it doesn't win you any prizes. You want that first meeting
to be as substantive and impressive as possible. The more tangible
information you give the client to take away, the better you will look
when he or she starts comparing you to the competition. Before you
can get to the nuts and bolts, first, like the old joke says, you have
to get their attention.

Sometimes the best attention-getter is the unexpected approach.
When we recruited Michael Jordan, we knew we were well posi-
tioned because we already represented a number of players who had
gone to the University of North Carolina, including several of Michael's former teammates. He probably already knew as much about
us as we knew about him.

We were the last to make a presentation that day, and I could see
that Michael was very tired, and probably sick of hearing the same
sort of spiel over and over again.

So I said, "Michael, I know you already know a lot about us. So
instead of telling you a lot of facts you already know, why don't we
use this time for you to ask questions—about us or about anything
else you've heard in other presentations today?"

Immediately, he perked up and we spent a very productive "conspiratorial" ninety minutes together, by the end of which we had already become his advisors in spirit, if not yet in fact.

In order to get a potential client's attention, I am not above using shock value if that's what it takes. There is probably no better example of this technique than the first meeting I ever had with Moses Malone.

Moses was a six feet eleven, seventeen-year-old black athlete from Petersburg, Virginia, and one of the greatest high school basketball players ever. One day Lefty Driesell, the coach at the University of Maryland, called me and said, "I've been recruiting Moses Malone for two years and now the Utah Stars have made him an offer to turn pro. It's a terrible offer, and I want you to come down and explain to him why it's a terrible offer and why he should go to college instead."

Lefty, of course, had more in mind than Moses' education and welfare. In fact, every day the lead sports story on page one in the Washington press was about Malone going to Maryland. MOSES TO LEAD MARYLAND OUT OF THE WILDERNESS, one headline read.

I went to the Marriott hotel in Arlington, Virginia, where Moses was staying. He was there with his mother, Mary Malone, Coach Driesell, and John Lucas, then a junior player at Maryland. Lefty met me in the lobby and gave me the Stars contract offer. I went off in the corner of the lobby to read it. I had about twenty minutes before I was to go upstairs to talk to Moses.

The contract was indeed a very unfair, one-sided deal. It was a four-year contract with *twelve* additional one-year contracts at the club's option. It was a potential sixteen-year contract for the best high school basketball player in America. I couldn't in good conscience recommend that he sign it. On the other hand, I certainly wasn't officially representing the University of Maryland either. It was also a sensitive PR matter because it meant so much to the community—my community—the Washington area. Before Lefty and I went upstairs I said to him, "I want to be clear with you, Lefty.

I'm a totally neutral third-party expert who is advising this kid on the pros and cons of this contract. I'm not representing Maryland. Do you understand?"

Lefty nodded, and we went upstairs to meet Moses.

As it turned out my concerns were almost beside the point. Moses was sitting on a couch, all knees and elbows, and Lefty said to him, "Moses, I want you to meet Mr. Dell."

Moses mumbled something. Though he did stick out his hand to shake, he was sitting down with his eyes staring straight at the floor. All these people were standing around. He was so painfully shy he couldn't even look up at me.

After talking a few minutes, I could see I was getting nowhere. He was so uncomfortable and nervous, he wasn't hearing a word I was saying. He just wanted this ordeal to be over with.

Finally, I said in a loud voice, "Moses, you ever heard of slavery?"

It was as if I had slapped him in the face. He looked up and stared straight in my eyes. "What did you say?"

"I said, have you ever heard of slavery? Because if you sign this contract that's virtual slavery. It could be for a total of sixteen years, and I've never seen a contract like that in my life."

"Fine," said Moses, "that's all I want to know."

Ultimately, Moses did turn pro shortly thereafter. We represented him, and he didn't sign any very one-sided sixteen-year contract. If I hadn't reached through to him that first time we met, it's hard to say whether or not he would have understood everything as rapidly.

Controlling the Meeting

When meeting with a prospective client, the overall aim is to make the biggest possible impact you can in the limited time available. The degree to which you succeed is directly linked to the control you are able to exercise over the meeting itself.

By controlling the meeting I mean *everything* about the meeting—from where it's held, to how long it lasts, from who or how many people may attend, to what's discussed.

I remember recruiting two basketball players at a college in the Midwest. I went into the meeting with three of my colleagues. The two athletes had an additional fourteen people in the room: parents, players, coaches, professors. It was a madhouse, and we didn't recruit the two kids.

Later, I heard one of the players had said of the meeting, "I felt Dell was cold and aloof." One of my strengths is my outgoing nature, but with that many people in the room I was just another face in the crowd.

We had too many people from ProServ there as well. The other player said, "I thought Dell was badly organized because he kept writing notes to his other people. If he had planned better, why would he need to write notes?"

In fact, I had written notes. I was so concerned with involving all of our people in the presentation, I was unaware of how it might look. My efforts were misunderstood, and backfired.

I learned from that experience. Most of the time when there are too many people, there is no relationship, no warmth, no one-on-one contact or feeling, no vibes. You're just part of a crowd. It doesn't work. There are, however, those unusual situations when it is necessary to make a statement about the size and strength of your organization. When we see this kind of situation facing us, we do march into the meeting in force—with lawyers, accountants, client managers, and so on. The key is to analyze the situation properly and to know which size group will be most effective.

Controlling the Agenda

To make the best use of meeting time you must control the meeting's agenda.

When recruiting clients, we'll generally have a typed-out agenda with us, which we will hand out when we arrive. A written agenda makes the client focus on the things *you* want to talk about. It is important, though, that the agenda anticipate the client's needs and concerns as well.

With any experience, it's fairly easy to know what the most likely questions and concerns are going to be, and to have your best answers ready. When we are recruiting a college basketball or football player, we will go through what it's like to be drafted, how the draft works, when the negotiations start, when the player meets the owner, what is a signing bonus, what is a playing bonus, what is a guaranteed no-cut contract, what are deferred payments. Then we will talk about financial management and taxes. Most client businesses are that way: The agenda may be different, but the client's likely concerns will usually be predictable.

With or without a written agenda, the most important thing to remember about controlling the meeting is that *it is not the person who talks the most who controls the meeting; it is the person who listens the most and asks the best questions.*

Just think of the most successful television talk shows: The host dominates and controls the show not by talking, but by asking questions and listening to answers. The direct benefits of talking less and listening more in meetings are numerous: It's how you get your information, it gives you time to think and react, and it lessens your chances of making a mistake, to name a few.

From the standpoint of courting new clients, the greatest advantage is that it allows you to tap into the meeting's "subtext"—all the vibes and subtleties which will strongly influence the meeting's ultimate outcome. You can't turn around a meeting that is not going well unless you are *aware* of the fact that it's not going well, and you are *aware* of the reasons why.

How do you limit your talking other than through sheer will-power? Like the talk show host, you ask questions and listen. Almost any comment you can possibly want to make or any point you want to get across can be phrased as a question, even if it's no more than, "What are your thoughts on . . . ?" rather than "I think."

Boomer Takes Charge

One reason I am so conscious of what it takes to control an initial meeting with a client is that I once had a prospective client totally turn the tables on me.

When Cincinnati Bengals quarterback Boomer Esiason was at the University of Maryland, he was one of the most sought-after seniors in the country. Over five hundred people had contacted him. After the season was over, he had narrowed it down to eight and invited them to meet with him during a two-day period. Our time was set at seven o'clock on a Tuesday night in the Maryland athletic offices at College Park.

We walked into the meeting, and Boomer said, "Very nice to meet you. I've heard a lot about you all and I hope you don't mind, but I have exams tomorrow and I really want to get back and study, so I'd like to tape our conversation. Then I can play it back at my leisure when I have time to evaluate your presentation."

We said fine. What else could we have said?

Boomer then brought out a list of questions, darn good questions, too, and just started firing them at us. "What are your fees? Why do you charge a percentage rather than an hourly rate?" He asked twelve to fifteen questions in all. Then he said, "That's everything I need to know. Thanks a million." We got up, shook hands, and left. The meeting lasted only about forty-five minutes.

On the way to our car I turned to David Falk and said, "That's the damndest meeting I've ever had. Either we have this player or we don't have any chance, but since *he* was so totally in control of the meeting, I don't have a clue which one it is."

We ultimately signed Boomer, and months later I asked him why he had conducted the meeting that way. "I was sick of the whole process," he said, "and wanted to get it over with as quickly as possible. Besides, I already knew a ton about ProServ anyway.

"The main reason I taped the meeting was because I wanted to compare everyone's answers to the same questions. Man," he added, "you can really tell the baloney artists and the guys who want to con you very quickly when you sit down and compare that way."

Boomer had it all planned. He had controlled everything, and we had to let him. We understood. We were smart enough not to fight upstream, though in a way we didn't really have much choice.

Chemistry

Obviously, the reason you want to control a meeting is that you are then better able to determine its outcome. What is more important than anything that is said is the chemistry which is developed. An ingredient of this chemistry involves first impressions, but it is much more than that. Good chemistry results from knowing how to make people become comfortable and interested.

A big problem for us is that many superstar college athletes, particularly those who have been heavily recruited and shielded by their coaches, aren't inclined to talk very much. They may be shy, or inarticulate, or maybe just sick of the whole process.

When you think about it, you can't really blame them. Selecting an agent (or a lawyer or broker or accountant—any of us) is not only a gamble, it's a hassle. Some of our clients have been burned before by people in our own profession.

You've got to get the client to open up—get his juices flowing—or you're dead.

When we run into this, we often use the same technique that Boomer Esiason used on us: We start asking a lot of questions. Where would you like to play? What do you think your strengths and weaknesses are as a player? What have you heard about this coach or that team? What are you looking for in a representative? Why did you happen to talk to us?

You have to create an informal conversational environment where there is a free flow of information. Communication is a two-way street.

You also have to establish a rapport with the client. I don't believe in those old salesman's tricks, like telling someone you like his tie or her dress. That's nonsense. Going into that first meeting with the client, I have prepared for it and know common areas of interest or will find them out quickly. If I'm recruiting a tennis player, for instance, I'm obviously going to talk a little tennis—strategy, philosophy, maybe about a match the client has recently played. By the same token, if you know your client collects antiques, races cars, loves to garden, or—the best—has children or grandchildren, *ask about those interests.*

Again, experience has taught me that you are far better off listening than talking. I'll ask clients a question and then sit back and let them talk. While they're talking I'm thinking, "How can I relate to what they're saying? What can I say to show them that I'm on *their* wavelength?"

At the end of the day, what it comes down to is: Did the client feel comfortable with you? Afterward, he or she doesn't sit around and say, "I think he understood my long-term cash flow needs" or "I liked his views on deferred compensation." What he says is, "I liked him" or "I didn't like him." Everything flows from this first impression.

Is this true of all clients or just pro athletes? Actually, it's true of all *people*. It's human nature to want to deal with people who make you feel comfortable and whom you like.

Think back a couple of years ago when Margaret Thatcher was the first Western leader to meet with Mikhail Gorbachev. Did she come out of that first meeting talking about his views on medium-range missiles in Europe? No. What she talked about was her impression of the man himself, and what she said was, "I can do business with that man."

When you get right down to it, that's exactly the feeling you want to leave behind. You want that client to say, "Now that's someone I can do business with."

Ending Meetings

I have lost clients because I have stayed in a meeting too long. By overtalking you can gild the lily. There is a sense of an ebb and flow in a meeting, and you want to leave on an "up" note. In addition, you never want the client to feel as if you're simply filling time.

Ending a meeting graciously and efficiently with a prospective client is the easiest thing in the world. Always phrase your wrap-up in deference to the client. You say, "I know you've got to get back to work," or "I know you've got a plane to catch," or "We didn't mean to take up so much of your time." End the meeting when *you* want to, but show deference to the client.

Selling a Service

Selling a service is a complex business because it doesn't have weight or measure. You can't touch it, you can't feel it, and you can't take it back for a refund. At the same time, the benefits of a service are not always readily apparent or can only be appreciated over the long term. Who, for instance, could possibly interview ten accountants and predict which one will save him or her the most over a period of ten years?

Make It Tangible

Although there is no substitute for establishing rapport with the client, you should also use whatever is at your disposal to make your services as real and tangible as possible. How effectively you are able to do this may well define the edge you have over your competitors who are still out there selling hot air.

We try to make our services concrete in several ways. We design and produce an attractive, informative marketing brochure in which we explain what we do for clients. Along with the brochure, we often include pertinent magazine and newspaper articles about our company or our other clients. In some cases, we will show brochures we have prepared for individual clients themselves. In particular, there is a brochure of Michael Jordan with a cover photo of him in a tuxedo that always seems to get a reaction. We also produce a glossy eight-page full-color newsletter reporting quarterly on all our clients' activities, copies of which we send to prospective clients.

Using television clips, we have produced a twelve-minute videocassette showcasing some of our clients and explaining our services further. On the tape some of our well-known clients talk about what we've done for them and their careers.

The key is to give clients something they can touch, something "real." Instead of attending an initial meeting with a client empty-handed, bring a written agenda to add a sense of real purpose and tangible work. By the way, if you're going to develop just one kind of public relations document or sales tool, make it a newsletter. A newsletter "proves" your expertise on an ongoing basis. For example, if you're a caterer, give recipes and entertaining ideas. Lawyers can offer invaluable updates on the changing law, as can accountants. Ad agencies can show off their best work and brag about new accounts. Your newsletter doesn't need to be full color, but do spend what it takes to get quality paper stock. You'll be surprised how impressed and appreciative your current and prospective clients will be!

A marketing plan which is customized to the particular client's needs and goals also makes for a strong impression at a first meeting. If you've been around for a while, if you know your business, and if you know what's doable for the client, this is a fairly straightforward document to construct and a very effective one to have in the initial meeting.

Set Yourself Apart

In keeping with earlier examples relating to getting the client's attention, you also want to do whatever you can to set yourself *apart* from the competition.

Often, we will be one of five or six people seeing an athlete one right after the other, all of whom begin to sound alike and probably even start to look alike to the client. Part of our job is to be different, to stand out from the competition.

Among the ways we have found to be most effective in putting our firm in a different, higher classification than our competition is by taking advantage of speaking and writing opportunities. You can do this, too. Make yourself available for panels at professional meetings. Contribute articles to publications. (Few things impress a prospective client more than a clipping from a magazine or newspaper which you have authored.) Particularly, learn to speak well in public, and do so at every opportunity.

Sell Your Track Record

Nothing makes a service appear more concrete than letting the prospective client know who your clients are and the kinds of things you've actually done for them.

When recruiting a college basketball player we often go into detail about what we've been able to do marketing Michael Jordan. Not only is Jordan one of the most spectacular, recognizable, and impressive players, but the licensing and merchandising campaign that has been built around him is the most successful in basketball history.

This prospective client may be talking to ten agents, and every one of them might be able to do for Michael Jordan what we did. But I know for a fact that we are the only one who actually represents Michael and who *has* done it, and it's our job to make sure the prospective client remembers that fact.

Since we've become internationally known, we try to elevate ourselves over the competition through our actual known results—what we have done and how well we've done it. That's why established businesses have a *competitive edge*. They have the powerful *advantage of precedent*. They can point to their clients and their successes. If you can show a top draft pick that you negotiated $30 million for Patrick Ewing, he's likely to say, "Gosh, if they did that for Ewing, I wonder what they can do for me?"

Potential clients often ask us to provide them with the names of other clients, which we're only too happy to do. But rather than give them two or three names, we'll give them a list of ten or twenty, all with home phone numbers. When you give them a list that long, you are already well on your way to establishing credibility.

Build a Network of Friends, Allies, and Confidants

In twenty years, one of the most intense competitions for a professional athlete I have ever been involved in was for Tracy Austin. At fourteen years old, she was already a champion and on her way to becoming America's darling—Chrissie Evert, Dorothy Hamill, and Mary Lou Retton all combined into one.

One of my real heroes and dearest friends is tennis legend Jack Kramer. I knew Tracy had grown up playing at the Jack Kramer

Tennis Club in Los Angeles. I also knew that for anyone with any sense of tennis history, his name is absolutely magic. When I was due to fly out to meet with Tracy and her parents, I called Jack and asked him to come with me. He agreed.

While we were sitting in Jeannie and George Austin's living room, Jack said, before I could even speak, "I want you to understand one thing about my being here. I am not objective on the subject of who should represent Tracy. If I had a daughter who was a great player, there is only one person in the world who I would ever want to represent her, and that's Donald."

We eventually represented Tracy, but Jack Kramer had gone to bat for me with such style and touch, I remember thinking to myself, "From here on it's just a matter of not messing it up."

When it comes to new client prospects, there is nothing more powerful than word of mouth. Nothing can top having people the client respects recommend you and say things about you which would sound conceited or obnoxious if you said them about yourself.

Over the years we have built up a network of allies throughout the sports world—coaches, sport officials, general managers, corporations, even television and newspaper people. This is our goodwill network. In any service business, there is nothing more important or irreplaceable. I would venture to say that over half our clients have been referred to us by someone within this people network.

This goodwill network also serves as our own early warning system. We try to stay close to the personal situation of as many prospective clients as possible, maintaining an information flow, trying to learn whether the rumors are true. There are rumors all the time. You hear, "So-and-so is going to sign with so-and-so," or "So-and-so just flew out to meet with what's-his-name."

Our network of friends is on the scene, out in the field every day. When Larry Brown was at Kansas, if we wanted to go after a Kansas player, we'd call Coach Brown and ask him if we had a chance. If he said, "Don't bother," we knew we could rely on that.

In almost any service business, it is your network of friends, allies, customers, and clients that give you your franchise.

Always Part on Good Terms

As a footnote to building a network of friends, it is best always to part with a client on good terms. Contact the client, tell him or her you're sorry it didn't work out, wish him or her good luck, and say that your door is always open—that if there is anything you could ever do for the client in the future, he or she should please let you know. A bitter or disgruntled former client can offset ten people who may say great things about you.

Closing the Deal

Too many people in client businesses are great at presenting their services but awful at closing the deal. They make their case and then wait around hoping the client chooses them.

That's not how it works. You have to be just as forceful in pressing for a decision as you were in presenting your case. Frankly, if I were the client, I wouldn't want anybody representing me who didn't know how to make someone commit or reach a decision.

You can be polite, but you have to be direct and you have to be firm. The best way to do this is not to force a final answer, but to make the client commit to a time when he or she will have an answer for you.

Sometimes you have to approach it from a number of different angles. We'll say, "John, have you reached a decision on who you want to represent you?" Most times the client will say no. Then you say, "What else can we do to answer your questions?" Or, "When are you going to decide?" Or, "Who is it between?" You want to leave the impression that it's time to commit: either to you or to someone else.

There are times when a prospective client begins to enjoy the recruiting process and drags it out as long as possible. You can end up wasting precious time chasing someone who has no intention of signing with you at all.

Sometimes parents, relatives, friends, and groupies love the recruiting process because they enjoy basking in the reflected glow of the attention being paid to the athlete. The players usually tire of it quickly, but the advisors often could let it go on forever.

When John McEnroe turned pro, everyone was recruiting him. It was a well-known joke that John's father went to dinner with about twenty different groups of agents and representative companies. The father loved the attention. He never once offered to pay for any of the entertainment—and then ended up representing John himself. I don't think he ever intended to do anything else.

Never Call Off the Chase

There is no shelf life to soliciting a client. Weeks, months, even years later after he or she has chosen someone else, the prospective client may become an actual client.

This has happened to us dozens of times. In one instance, a Pro-Serv executive sent tennis player Tim Gullikson a good luck telegram before one of his matches. That telegram made such an impression that three years later, when Tim decided to seek new representation, he signed with our company.

So never give up on a client. Too many people believe that sales is a do-or-die proposition but as long as you keep the selling process alive, you've got a chance at the business. A holiday greeting, relevant news clipping, get-well card, or note of congratulations keeps your name in front of a sales prospect and puts you and your firm in a favorable light.

This is another major reason why you never want to part with a client on bad terms. Ex-clients have a way of becoming clients again.

Several years ago the top-ranked black tennis player Zina Garrison left us because a black representative convinced her she would be better off without having to deal with the "color barrier." When that relationship didn't work out, she went to another black player representative. Meanwhile, Zina's representative at ProServ, Sara Fornaciari, had kept up with her and maintained her friendship. "Zina," Sara would tell her, "if you have a question or need advice, you can always call me. I'm your friend." It took a couple of years, but ultimately Zina decided that the person she trusted most was Sara, and she rejoined ProServ.

Never Assume You Know the Client's Decision

I usually have a feeling for what the client is going to do before he or she finally commits. But I've been wrong often enough to know not to bank on what I think is going to happen until it actually happens.

Two years ago Duke all-American Johnny Dawkins was slated to be a first-round basketball draft choice. We were told by his coach, Mike Krzyzewski, that Johnny was virtually committed to another firm. Nevertheless, since he was going to be in Washington anyway, would his coach mind, we asked, if we met with him?

The coach acquiesced, and when Johnny came to see us we decided to take our best shot. We said we thought he'd be drafted by either Chicago or San Antonio and that we had a very good working relationship with both teams—with Chicago because of Michael Jordan and with San Antonio because I'd known the owner, Angelo

Drossos, for years. Drossos is a proud Greek, and I told Johnny that I called him "Spiro," because he had shown ethnic pride when Agnew became Vice President, and after Agnew was indicted, I still called him "Spiro" to tease him. I wanted Johnny to know that Drossos and I were close enough to have that sort of relationship.

As it turned out, San Antonio did draft him in the first round, and ultimately, much to our delight, Dawkins changed his mind and went with us.

We've also been surprised the other way around. The year before we signed Dawkins, we really tried very hard to recruit a player from University of Kentucky by the name of Kenny Walker. The morning of the basketball draft we demonstrated our expertise to Kenny by telling him exactly where (fifth) and by whom (the Knicks) he was going to be picked.

It was like we had a crystal ball. When the Knicks took Walker, we said to ourselves, "He'll be playing for New York; he knows what we did for Ewing; he's our client."

And then he selected someone else.

Lose Graciously

Even when we lose a client, we want him or her to leave with a favorable impression of us.

We were about to go out to the University of Illinois to try to recruit quarterback Jack Trudeau when he called to say he was sick of the whole recruiting process, that he had narrowed the field to three agents, and that he didn't want to even meet us.

We told him, "We'd still like to see you get the best possible representation," and asked, "Who are the three?" One was Leigh Steinberg, who is an excellent agent. The second was a local guy, and the third was a pretty good negotiator.

We said, "We have nothing to gain by telling you this, Jack, but you can't do better than Leigh."

As it turned out, Jack didn't take our advice, but we wanted him to know that we had been impressed enough by him to want to steer him in the right direction.

The Last Impression

When the time comes for the client to commit, the impression you want to leave is obviously one of competence and comfort—that you are someone with whom the client will be able to relate to both personally and professionally.

There is a crucial piece of the puzzle still missing, and that piece is the question of character. In Chapter 1, I already stressed the need for honesty and integrity in dealing with clients. A person's character is also the underpinning of Chapter 3, which discusses the building of the client's trust and confidence. If I were the client, I would want to have a pretty good idea about a person's character before signing with him on the dotted line, rather than learning afterward.

Character is immutable. It can't change color with the situation. If there is the slightest doubt about a person's character up front, it will almost always come back to haunt you later on.

In any relationship where you are asking someone, in effect, to involve you in his or her personal affairs, your character must be beyond reproach.

Always Level with a Prospective Client Even if It Costs You the Client

When you're recruiting a major client sometimes it is easier to tell the client what he or she wants to hear rather than the absolute truth. The temptation is to rationalize: I'm not stretching the truth, I'm selling. Remember, the loss of one client or even a dozen clients is not worth the loss of your reputation.

Many of my recruiting techniques have been learned from college coaches, and I have been fortunate to learn from the very best, such as Dean Smith of North Carolina and John Thompson of George-town. Every year Dean and John speak with many of the top high school basketball players in the country, every year they absolutely level with these youngsters, and every year they lose a few good prospects as a result.

They will say, "This is a tough school, and you'll be expected to attend all classes and keep up your grade-point average to play on the team."

Or they will tell a high school player, "You may not start your freshman year. We have three seniors in front of you. But you'll become a better player by competing against them." The smart quality athlete knows he or she is hearing the truth, and respects that. If you think this honest approach doesn't pay, take a close look at Coach Thompson's and Smith's won-lost record.

Your client is paying you for your expertise. If you can't be straight with him or her, there's no way you can be effective.

Never Promise What You Can't Deliver

Remember, everything said during the recruiting and soliciting of clients has the permanence of having been carved in granite.

You never want to promise anything in the recruiting phase that you can't deliver later on. That doesn't just go for the income you feel you can generate or the job you think you can do. That goes for everything.

When Yannick Noah joined ProServ, Yannick's father, Zachary, who is a former professional soccer player in Cameroon and is now coach of the national team, said, "Mr. Dell, promise me one thing. Promise me you'll never spoil my son."

I replied, "Mr. Noah, I promise I will do my best never to spoil Yannick. But I can't promise you what the French public will do."

Four years later Yannick won the French Open in Paris, the first Frenchman to do so in fifty years, and the country went crazy. The evening after the finals, I saw Yannick's dad. "Well, Mr. Noah," I said, "I haven't spoiled him yet, but now France will."

I can also remember standing in Tracy Austin's living room the afternoon she turned pro. "Donald," Tracy said, "promise me that whatever happens, nothing will change."

I asked her what she meant, and she said, "I want to keep going to high school here in California. I don't want to travel a lot. I don't want you to schedule a lot of exhibitions for me. I want to play the circuit occasionally and go to school and be at home. I don't want my life to change just because suddenly a lot of money is involved."

I said, "Tracy, we won't schedule exhibitions, and we'll do everything possible to protect your privacy. But everything in life changes. You are a great tennis player, and like it or not, your life is going to change very quickly. I don't want you to hold it against me when it does."

Two years later Tracy at sixteen became the youngest U.S. Open champion in history and her life was never the same again.

In money matters I have found it dangerous to promise even what I think we can deliver. Success doesn't depend only on skill and talent. There are many factors you have no control over, such as the client's playing results, the economy, and whatever else goes in cycles or is in and out of fashion.

If you're confident you have the client committed, the best strategy is to promise less than you think you can deliver. Nothing gets a relationship off on the right foot faster than to promise X and deliver X, Y, and Z.

Finally, if a client is really trying to pin you down, you can always say, "I promise you I will always give you my best advice and my best judgment, and I promise you there will be no one who will work harder on your behalf."

Use the Available Facts to Your Advantage

Being truthful and leveling with the client doesn't mean "true confessions." You don't need to walk into your first meeting with a prospective client and confess how you blew this deal or screwed up that one. When recruiting clients, you don't score points with pity. Always remember that when all is said and done, you are still selling, so use the skill of positioning the facts to your best advantage.

If you've been recruiting a client for several years, and it comes time to fish or cut bait, stress the persistence, commitment, and dedication you've shown: The obligation the client should feel.

If a basketball player says to you, "You already have Ewing and Jordan. Will you have sufficient time and interest for me?" we will refer him to one of our other clients such as Adrian Dantley, John Lucas, or James Worthy, and suggest that he ask them if we have had the time and interest for them. We'll also point out the advantage of having the clout and leverage in the NBA that comes with representing clients like Ewing and Jordan.

You make the best argument for yourself that fits the facts . . . and you hope for the best.

CHAPTER THREE
"TRUST ME"

There is a game that children sometimes play where one child stands stiffly at attention, then slowly falls backward until caught by the waiting arms of a playmate. For the falling child the game is a test of mental strength. In order to maintain a straight-backed position he or she must have total trust and confidence in the playmate. If the falling child has the least bit of doubt in the playmate's skill (or intentions), the child will stick out an arm or a leg in order to break the fall.

Although this is a reasonably easy game for children to master, it is virtually impossible for adults. Adults, through their conditioning and their experiences, have learned not to trust anyone so totally. They would feel naive in doing so—and probably with good reason!

Yet until you earn the client's trust and confidence, you don't really have the client. It is trust and confidence that transform the commitment from a client into a relationship. Without it you are nowhere.

Trust and confidence. Fuzzy, cornball words, perhaps, but think back on your own experiences with anyone you have ever hired to do anything for you—from remodeling your kitchen to representing you in a legal matter—and you will see the correlation between the job that was done and the trust and confidence you placed in the person doing it.

The client's trust and confidence in you is also what allows you to get on with your work. Later, I will discuss at length how to deal with difficult clients. But it's worth noting here that if you don't have the clients' trust and confidence, *all* clients become difficult. When a client lacks trust in you and, as a consequence, is second guessing, criticizing, backbiting, or always ignoring your advice, there is no way you can get the job done properly. You waste time and effort, which invariably leads to resentment. Consequently, the client's trust in your integrity and abilities is what allows you to move forward confidently on the client's behalf.

Getting the trust and confidence of clients and customers is also how you build a business. A friend recently told me about taking his car to a new mechanic who had been recommended to him. Previous repair estimates had ranged up to $1,000 for a new valve job, but this mechanic took one look under the hood, reconnected a wire that had come loose, and sent my friend on his way with no charge. "Here was a guy I didn't even know," my friend said, "and now I would take anything he said about my car as gospel. He made a new customer for life." He had also made another emissary to spread the good word.

While getting my hair cut in New York recently, I was discussing with my barber the nature of his clientele. "Some people come in," he said, "and no matter what you do, they are not going to be happy.

They tell you what they want; you do exactly what they tell you, and then, if they don't like it, they blame you. When you ask them what it is they don't like, they say, 'I don't know. It just doesn't look right.'

"On the other hand, I have some customers who come in—usually they've been in a few times before—and I ask them what they want and they say, 'You're the doctor.' Whenever I hear that, I want to do my absolute best. These are the customers who become my long-term clients."

That, in a nutshell, is the relationship that you want to develop with clients. A client should believe that "you're the doctor." What you do might not be brain surgery, but the client's understanding and trust that you know more about your area of expertise than he or she does is what allows you to do your best work on the client's behalf.

The Bear and the Panda

How do you go about building trust and confidence? Generally it is a combination of professional performance and personal chemistry—how you feel about one another. Since no two clients will ever respond exactly the same way, there is no set formula. Perhaps there is no better illustration of this than our dealings over the years with the two major Communist superpowers. ProServ has been given the rare privilege of having business relations with Russia and China. In Russia, we represent the Russian Tennis Federation, for whom we have just negotiated a very capitalistic licensing agreement in apparel with Nike. In China, we have had a ten-year relationship, most recently as the official marketer of the upcoming "Asian Games," which China will be hosting in 1990.

An underlying sense of trust and confidence is obviously of the utmost importance in dealing with both countries. What struck both my associates and me was the dramatically different criteria by which trust and confidence is measured.

With the Russians, your reputation precedes you, so much so that it is the only reason that you are even invited to the bargaining table. With the Russians you have to be the leader in your field: the IBM of your particular industry. By the time we arrived, the Russians already knew as much about our accomplishments in tennis as we did. If we didn't have a track record we would never have been invited there. In fact, that track record began in 1961, when I became the first American to play competitive tennis in the Soviet Union.

Not surprisingly, the negotiating process with the Russians is extremely formal. Everything is very precise so that there is no room for misinterpretation in either Russian or English versions of the agreements. The whole process is very tedious; every *i* must be dotted and every *t* must be crossed. There is little extracurricular activity, no informal dinners, no parties, and minimal socializing before or after the negotiating sessions.

The Chinese, on the other hand, take a much more informal, relaxed approach. There is a great deal of entertaining, banqueting, and socializing. For the Chinese, past reputation means less; they judge you more for what you are, based on what they see. Are you, from their observations, someone they can trust? Are you, or will you become, a "friend of China"? It takes a long time to build a relationship to this level of trust, but once you are deemed to be a friend of China, you are a friend for life as long as you do nothing to violate that trust and confidence.

What's the best approach? Both have merit. Past performance is obviously a valid measure of future performance. And reputation will not only often get you in the front door, it will even get you some clients. Unless trust and confidence is based on more than that, you will only be as good in the client's eyes as whatever you've done for him or her lately.

If trust and confidence grow instead from the client's sense that you have his or her welfare and best interests at heart, then the bond is quite naturally going to be stronger than one based strictly on yesterday's performance.

Earning Respect

Unlike employees who newly join a company and are blessed with a kind of honeymoon period, I believe the honeymoon with clients is short lived or nonexistent. In fact, most new clients develop a kind of "show me" attitude.

This, to me, is a natural progression in the relationship. After the initial euphoria, a feeling-out period begins in which both sides, but particularly the client, hear this tiny voice saying, "Is this really going to work?"

At this point in the relationship the client might believe you are the right person for him; he or she may even like you. But trust is built on respect, and respect comes not from how well respected you might be by others but from how you perform for that particular client.

Until you've earned that respect through performance, that little voice in the back of the client's mind is going to keep yapping away.

Make Something Happen—Quickly

There are no shortcuts to getting the client's respect. There's no secret to it either: It comes from delivering, making something happen for the client, fast. In my business, nothing gets you on the track faster and in better shape with a client than doing a quick deal.

When tennis player Eliot Teltscher originally came to us he had previously been represented by one of our competitors. They hadn't gotten him as much money from outside endorsements as he had hoped. He was a personable, good-looking American player. We were pretty confident we could do a good job for him. Based on our assurances, he joined us. Within thirty days we got him a racquet, a shoe, and a clothing contract. These deals said to him, "You made a good decision to come with us. We promised that you would make money. Here it is, done already."

If you can't make a big deal then make a little one. If we don't see a major licensing or endorsement deal on the near horizon, we will quickly put the client into an exhibition match or arrange a one-shot personal appearance fee. The client is so sensitive to your performance in the initial days and weeks of representation, there is something to be said for subscribing to an "any deal in a storm" philosophy.

Even putting together a proposal or a status report or a memorandum on a "crazy new idea" can get the excitement and credibility going.

Put yourself in the client's shoes. You can make all the promises you want; you can explain why you're the best person for the job; you can cite your track record. But when all is said and done, until you show tangible results it's all just so much hot air.

Making a deal, of course, is the quick pick-me-up for any time during the life of a client relationship. Well into our representation of Arthur Ashe, who was quite busy with television broadcasting and his responsibilities as Davis Cup captain, we felt more responsibilities might spread him too thin.

However, I began sensing from Arthur that he might like to do even more. I then sat down with Arthur and discussed just how many new commitments he would like to take on. With this information, we then developed relationships for him with such blue-chip companies as Aetna, Visa, and Bristol Myers.

This increased commercial activity was good for Arthur. He did a great job for these companies and felt increasingly good as a businessman.

Show Results in Other Ways

Someone asked me recently how I would handle a client like John McEnroe. My response was, "I'd get him five public service TV spots." Right now, his image is so negative that it really hurts his merchandising opportunities. Anything I could quickly do to improve his public image would be much more valuable to him in the long run than big-number endorsement deals we might be able to pull off for him.

If you can't make a deal right away, you can still start to build the client's respect by advising him in ways that immediately show positive results.

When we first represented tennis great Jimmy Connors, he had a bad boy reputation. Most fans loved him, but others were offended by his ill-tempered outbursts on the court, and it was costing him a great deal of money. Companies who should have been using Jimmy in commercials had been steering clear of him for fear he would do something outrageous on the court and maybe embarrass them.

When we began representing Jimmy in 1983, he was no longer a teenager. He was married, with a family, and we felt he needed to tone down his on-court behavior. We told him, "We can build a public relations campaign around you that will not only change your image but bring you a great deal more money from corporate sponsors.

"But," we added, "we can't do it alone. We need your help and cooperation." Jimmy agreed. He stopped his temperamental outbursts on the court, became more cooperative and open with the press, and associated himself more publicly with a few charities he had been helping privately. We also stressed the strong family values which he inherited from his mother, Gloria, and which have grown since his marriage to Patti.

During the next several years, Jimmy signed substantial endorsement deals with corporations like the Paine Webber brokerage house and Sony. He has become not only one of the most popular players in the game today but also one of the most financially successful.

I can also remember when we signed a young tennis player by the name of Brad Gilbert. He was having trouble winning because as far as we were concerned he kept changing his schedule, putting himself in the wrong tournaments, and playing too often around the world at the wrong times. For months we kept telling him this, and he kept ignoring our advice. One year at Wimbledon we told him he might be better off with another representative, since it was clear he didn't seem to trust our judgment enough to heed our advice.

He was so surprised he altered his plans and agreed to our proposed schedule. Three weeks later he won his first tournament. Once that happened, he began to take our advice seriously on almost everything else. He finally realized that we did know a little something about the game and that we had his best interests at heart.

Showing results through advice can be a tricky business, particularly at the outset when the client has less reason to trust your wisdom than he or she would later on. It's important to make sure the client understands the specific results that your advice is intended to achieve.

For instance, early in our relationship with Olympic volleyball star Karch Kiraly, we were negotiating an endorsement deal with a national watch company. It was not for a great deal of money, but we thought the deal would be good for Karch, who needed the exposure.

Karch was looking only at the short term—the money in the deal—which didn't impress him. We had to fight hard to convince him that the important consideration was not the money but rather the national exposure the deal would give him. "You may be the best volleyball player in the world," we told him, "but no one knows you. You have to get your name and face out in front of the public."

Karch finally relented, accepted the deal, and the watch company eventually used his picture in store displays which appeared in six hundred Athlete's Foot stores across America. You can't buy that kind of publicity. The campaign was so successful that this initial commitment led to more lucrative financial opportunities elsewhere.

Good advice is a valuable commodity in every business situation and can help build a solid relationship with a client. Our television company was recently working with a corporation that had a new product to introduce. They were anxious to roll out a national campaign and wanted ProServ Television to produce an expensive commercial which would be the cornerstone of the campaign for the new product.

Producing the costly commercial would have been a lucrative piece of business for us, but Bob Briner, the president of our television company, convinced the company to use some much less expensive spots to run on local cable systems in order to test the best advertising approach before committing to the much more expensive production.

At first the president and vice president of marketing for the company could not believe we were advising against producing the national spot with all the expensive bells and whistles, but when they thought it over, they recognized the soundness of the advice and saw that we were interested in building a long-term relationship rather than in making a quick buck.

For Now, Give It a Shot

If you can't arrange a quick deal or show tangible results in other ways, the next best thing is to show the client that you're in the arena—that you're out there making your best effort for him or her.

The better you understand your business, the more you know up front what can be done and what is a waste of time. A client says,

"What about this . . . ?" or "Why don't we try that . . . ?" and a little voice goes off inside saying, "That will never work." Usually, that's the voice of experience. Down the road the client might very well be willing to listen to that voice of experience. But not up front. You have, after all, been hired to "do something" and it is crucial at this stage of the relationship that you be perceived to have a can-do attitude even if deep down inside you might think you're wasting your time.

Also, in our business—and I think this is true of many client businesses—we sometimes have a tendency to outguess ourselves and rationalize that something is not going to work only because we don't want to commit the necessary up-front time to find out. Yet most of the major licensing and endorsement deals that we have done started out as no's—which, through persistence and determination, we turned into yesses.

Negativity breeds inactivity under any circumstances. With a client who has yet to learn to trust your judgment in these matters, you are far better off making the effort and failing than not making the effort at all.

To Tell the Truth

One of the greatest dangers in dealing with clients is telling the client what he or she *wants* to hear, rather than what is in his or her best interest. This is a particularly difficult situation when a client has not yet reached the point of totally trusting your advice or respecting what you say.

You must always level with the client, but how you say it—how you couch it—varies with how well you know the client and the degree to which he or she respects your opinion.

I can remember trying to convince a tennis-playing client that he had to get rid of his coach. The coach was using the player for his own purposes. We knew it, the coach knew that we knew it, and even the player knew it. There was a real risk that we were going to lose the client because it really came down to choosing between us and the coach, and it was the coach with whom the player had had a long personal history.

What we ended up doing was having several discussions with the player over a period of time, and each time we became less circumspect in our feelings. By the time we made it a him-or-us issue, we were pretty sure he would accept our advice and get rid of his coach, which he did.

To gain the client's respect, and to keep it, you have to always tell the truth, even when it hurts and even at the risk of losing the client.

I once had to say to one of our female tennis clients, "I'm going to tell you the unpleasant truth. How are you going to be a top ten player when you are fifteen pounds overweight?" That's real honesty. "Remember when Martina Navratilova was chubby?" I added. "She's not fat now, and she's number one. Name one player in the top ten who's even three pounds overweight." The client didn't like hearing that, but she respected me for saying it.

Are your clients spreading themselves too thin? Have they crossed some professional line and gotten themselves into trouble? Are they making life miserable for their co-workers, or for you? If you want the relationship to last beyond the honeymoon, you've got to be able to deal straight with your clients and give them the good news, the bad news, and the hard news.

Getting to Know the Client

We are in the business of getting personal. It is one of the reasons we spend hours with our clients. When you first meet a client, you can't just push a button and become bosom buddies. You have to make the effort. You work with the client on the telephone. You travel with him or her to meetings. And then, when the critical moment comes to make a tough decision, you can make it knowing the client will back you up.

The relationship between the representative and the client often has to be built quickly. With our basketball clients, for instance, we sign a player in June, and by August or September we are asking him to sign a multimillion-dollar contract. We then ask him to trust us in making some of his life's most important decisions. If he wants to get married, should he have a prenuptial agreement? How much money should he give to his immediate family? Should he buy them a house or a car? Should he put them on an allowance? Would that undermine their dignity about working? These are important decisions that we are helping a virtual stranger make for himself. We are asking for a lot of trust in a very short period of time.

I suppose it is possible to gain some trust merely by knowing your business. Without knowing the client at all you can look at what a tennis player is doing and say to yourself, "He (or she) is never going to win playing this schedule." Over the long haul, there is absolutely no way to gain the trust and confidence of clients without getting to know them well. So much of what you do is contingent upon the client's own unique personal makeup—his or her likes and dislikes, wants and needs, and good points and bad. Unless you and the client are in agreement as to where you are going, you are almost certainly going to end up in different places.

To get to know our clients we initially spend as much time with them as our mutual schedules will permit. Sometimes at a meeting we will spend all of our time talking about the client's personal problems: his or her current life, parents, spouse, or boy- or girl-friend. Often this will make business a lot easier to get done later on because the client knows that we have his or her best interests at heart, and that we can be relied upon. By putting in the time, we also show the client we care.

Sometimes in getting to know the client, you may not like what you find out. But if you and the client are going to see eye to eye, you have to know his or her weaknesses as well as strengths.

Ivan Lendl, for instance, is not big on small talk or social niceties. If you understand what he doesn't like to do, such as speaking engagements or socializing at cocktail parties, you know what companies can and cannot expect of him, and you adjust the commitment you make for him accordingly.

We designed Ivan's contracts in such a way that very little was expected from him in the way of personal appearances. If he did more, fine. Then he looked like a hero. If we did a normal contract with the usual number of appearances, he might look as if he were not performing.

With this strategy we were able to fulfill Lendl's desires without injuring his credibility with a company for which he was working. Several years ago, for instance, we made a two-year deal with Avis that called for Lendl's likeness to be used in an ongoing billboard campaign. The arrangement also called for a minimal number of personal appearances on Avis's behalf.

The first year the billboards were up, Lendl lost only three matches the entire season and went from second in the world to number one, which was great for a company that has built its entire "We Try Harder" advertising campaign around being number two. If the agreement had been based on more appearances, Ivan would have been unhappy, as would have Avis. Instead, the focus was on Lendl's tennis success, and by extension, the success of their billboard campaign. As far as Avis was concerned, Lendl had delivered more than they had contracted for. When it came time to renegotiate, they happily extended this contract for more money.

In getting to know Jimmy Connors and in getting him to trust us, one of the key elements was understanding his inherent mistrust of others. For most of Connors's career, he has been pulled this way and that by people who want to be known for knowing Jimmy

Connors. Consequently he is very suspicious of situations involving even the hint of "groupieism."

As a result, in the first year of our agreement with McDonald's, Jimmy's six-figure contract called for only one personal appearance, which McDonald's thought was crazy. We told McDonald's, "Trust us. Jimmy will do more than one appearance, but only if he is required contractually to appear just one day." As it turned out, Jimmy being Jimmy, he did many Ronald McDonald House charity appearances, not because he had to, but because he *wanted* to. If he had done them only because of a contractual obligation, he would have done them grudgingly, and McDonald's wouldn't have gotten nearly as much PR for their money.

Trust by Association

One of the reasons we try to turn the key advisors of our clients into long-term allies is that they often have a perspective the client doesn't—an objectivity about the relationship. If the client sees that someone he or she trusts has trust in us, it often becomes a matter of "trust by association."

Frankly, when we negotiated Patrick Ewing's contract with the Knicks, we didn't know Patrick that well. Patrick is private and shy, and initially we didn't want to push ourselves on him. Fortunately, we had enough experience to anticipate what these negotiations would be taking out of him and the good sense to involve someone whom he already knew and trusted.

To put the situation in perspective, here was a young man who had starred at Georgetown University for three years and had led the team to a national championship in his junior year. He was inundated with "free advice" telling him that he should turn pro immediately and cash in. Obviously, he was worth millions of dollars to virtually every team in the NBA. At the same time, he did not come from a wealthy background. People were challenging him, saying, "If you stay at Georgetown for your senior year, you stand to risk losing millions of dollars. What happens if you tear up your knee?"

Patrick felt strongly about obtaining his college degree. He enjoyed a very close personal relationship with his coach, John Thompson, and felt a special sense of loyalty to him. John, in fact, enlisted our opinion regarding Patrick's turning professional at the conclusion of his junior year. We later found out that ProServ was the only representative in the country that had advised Patrick to remain at Georgetown. I do not know what factors ultimately helped Patrick to decide, but as it turned out, he did return to Georgetown for his senior year, after which he was overwhelmingly acclaimed as the top player in the country.

In 1985, the NBA instituted a new lottery system to determine which of the seven teams that did not qualify for the playoffs has the right to select first in the annual NBA college draft. The New York Knicks won the lottery and on June 18, 1985, drafted Patrick number one in the entire NBA draft. The "experts" predicted that Patrick would receive a contract ranging between $1.2 million to $1.5 million per year for several years. Based upon the lottery, Patrick's talents, and the Knicks' disastrous 1983–84 and 1984–85 seasons, we felt that Patrick had a unique value and were determined to wait the Knicks out until he received it.

Instinctively, I knew this was going to create a problem: Would Patrick lose confidence in us when we recommended that he turn down all of the money that would be immediately dangled in front of him? There was only one person in the world who could help us in this situation. Therefore, I went to Patrick's coach and mentor, John Thompson, and explained our strategy to him and our concerns. Thompson assured us that he would do everything he could to assist us if it would benefit Patrick.

When Patrick was interviewing potential representatives, Coach

Thompson had told him, "Remember that representing players is a profession just like coaching or playing ball. Hire the people you feel will do the best job for you and *then let them do their job.* You hired these guys for their expertise . . . *listen to them.*" And he did. Patrick held firm even when the New York Knicks first offered him $1.2 million in cash per year. When we finalized Patrick's contract for more than $3 million per year, we felt that ProServ had come a long way toward earning Patrick's trust. His Knicks contract paid him the highest salary in the history of team sports.

Getting to know the client in order to earn his or her trust or confidence is hardly unique to the business of sports representation. All the time I see lawyers who just assume their job is merely to "protect the client" without any understanding of the degree to which the client wishes to be protected. A client is only 100 percent protected by never making a deal. Most good businesspeople are willing to take reasonable risks. It is only by knowing where an individual client fits on the risk/reward scale that a lawyer can give his or her client the kind of advice the client needs rather than the kind of advice the lawyer *thinks* the client needs.

Making Friends out of Clients

Everyone has heard that old adage "Never do business with friends or relatives." Though I've worked closely and well at ProServ with my brother, Dick, ever since he retired from the pro tour, and though I've represented my dear friend Jack Kramer in numerous business deals (admittedly Jack doesn't like to pay fees), I suppose the reason that the maxim is repeated so often is that there is some truth to it.

Indeed, I have seen many, many young athletes end up mistaking loyalty for trust, and friendship for obligation. They agree to let a friend or relative manage their careers and end up losing themselves millions of dollars and a lifetime of security, and experiencing a family rift as a result.

What amazes me is how often people will misinterpret this adage to mean, "Don't *make* friends out of the people with whom you do business." For any business involving clients, that attitude can be fatal.

The aim of any "people business"—and what business really isn't about people—should be to develop a personal as well as a professional relationship with the people with whom you are working. I'm not suggesting that you should try to turn everyone into your best friend, but there are all levels of friendship. I do think that you should try to attain whatever levels of friendship you can, within the limits of the business relationship.

"Don't Take It Personally, But . . ."

Making friends out of clients is the graduate school of client management. The emotional stakes go up on both sides. The more personal the relationship, the greater the rewards and the deeper the wounds.

I once had the father of a tennis client come to me and say that his daughter was going to resign from our firm. I had been very close to the entire family, and the father felt very uncomfortable telling me this. I didn't make his task any easier.

About halfway through the father said to me, "Donald, please don't take any of this personally. You know how much we like you. It's just business."

I blew up. "Don't tell me how I'm supposed to take it," I said. "I do take it personally. We've worked our butt off for your daughter, put our heart and soul into it, and now you tell me I'm not supposed to take it personally. That's baloney." I was very upset and hurt, which is the price you sometimes have to pay in the personal service business.

Do you remember the line in *The Godfather* just before one of the Godfather's lieutenants is about to blow away his longtime friend who had betrayed the family? "It's just business," he says.

It's a nice line, but totally lacking in truth. One of the great business lies is that business is ever "just business." Any personal service business is *always* personal and anyone who believes otherwise is just engaging in a convenient self-deception.

In fact all business could benefit from opposing sides taking a little more time to get to know one another. I was struck recently by a *New York Times Magazine* story on the unlikely alliance between General Motors and the United Auto Workers union, from which the following passage is taken:

> The U.A.W.'s bargaining team and G.M.'s top negotiators had gone off together to Japan. During their visit the two groups toured factories together, took meals together, went drinking together, even shopped together. Back in Detroit, the talks went far more smoothly than the experts had anticipated. The union did not even have to set a strike deadline. An agreement emerged that both sides praised as launching a new joint effort to turn G.M. around. "The trip," recalled G.M.'s vice president, "had given us an opportunity to develop a trusting relationship before going to the table."

The Comfort Zone

If befriending your clients can sometimes lead to bitter disappointment, why even take the risk? Because the rewards in both personal and business terms are so much greater. From a purely business standpoint, a friendship with a client pays off by creating a large comfort zone in which to work.

A comfort zone is the area of client communications in which you don't have to look constantly for hidden meanings in what the other is saying. The greater the comfort zone, the more honest and direct you can be with the client, and the client with you. You don't have to play games, you can open up to each other, and you can air your grievances without rancor or suspicion. As a result you can be more effective for the client and for yourself.

You establish a comfort zone with a client by getting personal. For instance, I intentionally try to form a teasing relationship with clients because I know that if I can joke and tease with them, our relationship has a safety net. When things get awkward or uncomfortable, or when something difficult needs to be discussed, or even when the relationship is going through one of its inevitable strains, zinging each other or getting the other person to laugh or see him or herself in a less serious way is a great tension reliever. Teasing and joking is how I show affection, and the need for affection is a powerful human need.

Once I get close to a client, the teasing can become even more sharp and personal. When I played on the tennis circuit everyone loved to needle each other. It was just something you did to "belong."

Jack Kramer is a tremendous needler, funny and sarcastic, and I love to needle him back. Whenever I call his home, I ask to speak to "Czar-baby," since for years when he ran the Association for Tennis Professionals he was called the czar of tennis. Immediately the Kramers know who it is on the other end of the line, which sets the friendly tone for the phone conversation to follow.

Even something as seemingly innocuous as a nickname can have a powerful effect. With Arthur Ashe, for instance, I would always call him "lieutenant" during our Davis Cup days since he was a second lieutenant "on loan" from the U.S. Army. Years later, when Arthur suffered a particularly bitter defeat at Wimbledon, I left a note in his Westbury hotel box that read, "Lieutenant: There'll be other days and other victories." Arthur told me later that when he saw himself referred to in that manner, "Lieutenant," he smiled at the thought of the "good old days" of our Davis Cup team experiences and began to put his loss back into perspective.

It is with Arthur and Stan Smith, two clients with whom I've had the longest relationship, that I have the greatest comfort zones. Over the years the three of us have built up an entire shorthand language between us. It is a potent form of communication because it allows us to discuss potentially loaded subjects in a nonexplosive way.

Several years ago I woke up to a headline in *The Washington Post* which read, ARTHUR ASHE SUED BY SBA [SMALL BUSINESS ASSOCIATION]. That was news to me, but when I called Arthur he explained that he had cosigned a promissory note for his old friend and first tennis teacher, Ron Charity, and that Charity had defaulted on the loan.

I was upset and wanted to sue Charity. But Arthur felt he "owed Charity one" and insisted that he would pay off the loan himself. I was determined not to acquiesce without getting something straight between us.

"All right, Arthur," I said, "I'll respect your decision in this case, but in the future if I ever say to you, 'This is one of those Ron Charity deals,' then that means we don't do it, okay?" From that day on, Arthur and I added another shorthand phrase to our repertoire and a better way of doing business as a result.

Our deep and wide comfort zone has allowed us to resolve a number of potentially uncomfortable situations amicably. In the early 1970s, for instance, when Ashe was at the height of his popularity, he was beginning to use his status and reputation in the tennis world to advance black causes. That was understandable, but when Arthur announced he was going to play an exhibition match to raise money for the Black Panthers, I knew that his image as a corporate spokesperson and endorser of products would suffer greatly as a result. While I sympathized with Arthur's point of view, I also had to be very direct with him. "Arthur," I said, "the majority of white

Americans feel threatened by the Black Panthers. There is no way you can endorse them without severely hurting yourself with the American public." Instead, we came up with a systematic plan for Arthur to financially support a number of worthwhile black causes and organizations, rather than just the Panthers.

My deep and wide comfort zone with Stan Smith once helped me resolve a very sensitive matter with Stan regarding his father. Stan's father was an attractive and friendly gentleman who was justifiably very proud of Stan and all he had accomplished in tennis. The elder Mr. Smith had been a California high school physical education teacher all his life. Understandably, his knowlege of sports representation and marketing was limited. This limitation did not deter him from taking an intense interest in the job we were doing for Stan and particularly in the ways we were investing Stan's money.

After a while, the father's interest became so intense and meddlesome that it affected our ability to do a good job for his son. We were spending so much time with the father justifying our marketing efforts and investment decisions that there was little time left to be effective for Stan.

Needless to say, this was a delicate problem, but one that had to be addressed. With some fear and trepidation, I approached Stan about the situation. I was careful to emphasize how much I liked his dad. Also, I wanted to be sure that Stan knew that we were always willing to discuss his situation with him or anyone he designated and that his investment accounts were always open for review. I also explained to him, however, that all the time we were spending answering his father's numerous queries had a negative effect on our ability to do a good job for him.

Stan picked up on what I was saying right away. He immediately said, "Donald, don't worry about my dad. I will take care of it." From that point on, the relationship with his father was never a problem again.

The Acid Test

One of the big-time energy wasters in dealing with clients is playing mind games with yourself: "If I say *this,* will he think or do *that,*" and so on. With a wide comfort zone you don't have to be second, third, or fourth guessing yourself constantly. You can be less calculating and more direct.

I do not mind, for instance, asking the clients whom I consider friends for personal favors, sometimes to the consternation of some of our associates. Admittedly, this flies in the face of a lot of conventional client-management wisdom: If a client does you a personal favor you are more "beholden" to him or her in some way. But to me this is the acid test of a real friendship with a client. It takes the quid pro quo—the scorekeeping aspect—out of the relationship.

Recently I had to cancel a trip to Atlanta, Georgia, where I was scheduled to do some television commentary for a tournament there. I knew that Jimmy Connors was going to be in Atlanta making an endorsement appearance. I called him at the last minute, told him my problem, and asked him to replace me in the broadcast booth. He was only too happy to oblige. Did Jimmy feel I "owed him one" for this? I doubt it. I'm not a scorekeeper, and neither is Jimmy. In any event, the matter has never come up since my call.

Little Things Mean a Lot

The key to earning a client's friendship—and by extension the client's loyalty—is to show him or her that he or she is more than a meal ticket for you—that you have the client's personal and emotional welfare at heart as well as his or her wallet. You have to show the client you *care.*

In this respect, never overlook the power of the small personal gesture—the birthday call, the get-well card, the acknowledgment of special life events such as weddings and anniversaries.

It isn't necessary for the gesture to be some thought-out pre-planned activity. There is great mileage to be gained from a quick cup of coffee, a beer at the bar, or a five-dollar, fifteen-minute, fast-food lunch. It can be any spur-of-the-moment thoughtfulness. I was once having dinner with Yannick Noah in Lusanne, Switzerland. During the course of the evening he mentioned that his wife would be celebrating her birthday the next day. I made a mental note, and I called her from the Paris airport the next day to wish her a happy birthday. From the pleasure and surprise I heard in her voice, I could tell that my birthday call was something she would remember. The point is that, when these things occur to you, don't dismiss them or talk yourself out of making these little thoughtful gestures. They can be all-powerful when it comes to building friendship within the constraints of business relationships.

When our clients are abroad, I also like to send them telexes or faxes to congratulate them on victories or to pump them up the evening before a match. To me, a telex in writing has more of an impact than most forms of communication, and it shows that I am thinking of them.

A few years ago, when I realized the power and significance of these simple, unexpected acts of consideration, we hired some additional people as administrators primarily to handle clients' special requests and out-of-the-ordinary needs. I can't tell you how many times the "little deal" we were able to make for a client has come back to reward us in loyalty and friendship. Seven-figure contracts come and go, but getting a client a free flight or a free vacation package in Barbados? Now that's something to remember!

Being There

Obviously, I strongly endorse turning clients into friends. If you choose to take this approach, there is one caveat: *You can't fake it.*

Like everything else in life worth having, friendship comes with a price. You have to make the effort. Sometimes you have to overlook certain things, sometimes you have to be forgiving, and all the time it has to be real. If you are perceived by the client to be a part-time or "sunshine" friend, then any trust you have built up will evaporate. In fact, it's as if a big minus sign has been put up in front of all your prior dealings. The greater the trust has been, the more let down the client feels and the more distrustful he or she becomes.

Part of the price is "being there" for the client at those moments in the relationship when you really have to be there. Usually, these are moments of crisis when clients in their personal or business life need a shoulder to lean on or a word of condolence, or maybe just someone to encourage them. At the same time, don't forget to celebrate moments of shared happiness or victory.

A couple of winters ago one of our client managers had made vacation reservations for himself and his wife a full four months in advance of a prestigious tennis tournament he assumed one of his clients would never even qualify for. Not only did the client qualify, he made it all the way to the finals. When the client reached this high point in his career, his representative knew his rightful place was to be at the tournament giving him moral support. He literally left his wife by the pool and flew back to watch his client play in the finals of the tournament.

One of the most difficult periods of my life occurred when Arthur Ashe underwent a serious heart operation. When I heard about it, I dropped everything I was doing, canceled my schedule, and Carole and I went to the hospital to be at Arthur's side. Everything else in my life came to a screeching halt as I devoted my energies to Arthur and his wife, Jeannie, and his dad until I was certain he was okay. I cannot think of anything else in my life that would have taken precedence over this, save a personal family crisis. Given my relationship with Arthur, this is hardly surprising, but that's the point: I feel this way not because he is a trusted client, but because he's a *trusted friend.*

Personal Chemistry:
The Right Mix

It would be misleading to suggest that if you do the job for clients, make an effort to get to know them, and extend yourself every once in a while on their behalf, the relationship is always going to work.

This formula will work most of the time, but there are also any number of intangible factors which collectively can be referred to as "chemistry." If the chemistry isn't right between you and the client, then trust and confidence will never emerge and your advice will always be suspect. When this is clearly the case, it is best just to cut your losses and go your separate ways.

This rarely happens to us, but one case I can remember quite vividly was our representation of basketball star Bernard King. As an all American at the University of Tennessee, Bernard had gotten into some trouble with alcohol and the law. We were given a strong indication that underneath it all, Bernard wasn't such a bad guy. After some internal discussion and doubt, we took him on as a client.

Almost from the beginning the chemistry between us wasn't very good. Early on he rented a high-rise apartment in Guttenberg, New Jersey, on a short-term lease. He called us one day and told us he was hiring a decorator to fix up the apartment. He said he thought it was important that after working so hard he come home and unwind in surroundings he enjoyed.

We agreed and asked him what he thought it was going to cost. "I've already checked," he said. "It'll cost about forty-seven."

"Forty-seven sounds a little high," we said. "Try keeping it to about twenty-five hundred. Buy a bed, and you can rent the rest of the furniture."

Bernard hesitated a moment and said, "You don't understand. Not forty-seven hundred. Forty-seven thousand!"

We hesitated a moment and said, "Bernard, you can't spend forty-seven thousand dollars decorating a *rented* apartment. You might be traded to another city in two months. That's why you have a short-term lease. This is a total waste of money."

When the decorator's proposal came to us, we called Bernard. We said, "Bernard, what's going to happen to all this stuff when you move out?" He said, "I'll take it all with me." We answered, "You can't take one-hundred-dollar-a-yard wallpaper with you. You can't take wall-to-wall carpeting." We got the expense down to about $14,000. Every exchange we had was a personal challenge to him, and he began to resent us. Bernard saw us as underestimating his intelligence and knocking him for making a bad financial decision.

A few months later, Bernard called to say he was moving out. He had found another apartment. "Where are you moving?" we asked. "I'm renting an apartment that has a better view of the river," he answered, *"in the same building."*

We threw up our hands. We were wasting our time and his money, paying us for advice he never followed.

I was also concerned about Bernard's going bankrupt. If that happened, the finger of blame would be pointed directly at us. I felt we could not risk exposing our company in that manner, and suggested he get a new representative.

It was unfortunate, because he's a great player who has had a great career. But the communication or chemistry was wrong between us. Our aims for him always clashed with what he wanted to do.

That and similar experiences left me with the belief that though everyone deserves good representation, a lawyer/agent can only do a good job for a client where there is at least some foundation of trust and confidence. The relationship is too much of a marriage to work without it.

Life is too short to be locked in a relationship with someone whom you must battle every step of the way. Often it's just easier, for you and for the client, to part company. If I'm going to knock myself out for a client, I'd rather do it for a client who believes in us.

CHAPTER FOUR

GETTING ALONG WITH CLIENTS

When it comes right down to it, there is very little mystery about getting along with clients. All you have to do is figure out exactly what they want and then give it to them twenty-four hours a day, seven days a week. Since this, of course, is neither doable nor desirable, the next best thing is to make sure that you and the client have a clear understanding of what each can and cannot reasonably expect from the other.

Getting Yourself on the Same Page

Several years ago, shortly after we had taken on a new tennis client, we started getting phone calls from him asking us to line up practice partners at the various tournament sites.

At first we thought he just didn't know the other guys on the tour well enough to arrange his own practice dates, and we were happy to make the introductions. It began to dawn on us that he thought this was part of our job as his representative: to bring in income through licensing and endorsements, to manage his business affairs and personal finances—and to find him practice partners.

In fairness to the client, the fault lay more with us than with him. We had failed to communicate clearly to him the scope of our duties and responsibilities. He had his agenda, we had ours, and the way the relationship was actually supposed to function fell somewhere in between.

A client's clear understanding of what you can and cannot do, and what you are and are not willing to do, is essential to a smooth working relationship. Without it, you and the client will often be working at cross purposes, and the relationship will be frustrating for both of you.

Establishing Clear Goals

I have found the best way to assure that you and the client are both rowing in the same direction is to establish clear-cut, mutually agreeable short- and long-term goals. Not only do clear-cut goals give you something to shoot for and a tangible measurement of performance, but they keep you from going off on tangents. With mutual goals, you'll move forward together.

Establishing specific and clear-cut goals also gives you a blueprint for what you're attempting to accomplish just as a blueprint helps an architect to communicate with the builder and the contractor. It acts as a point of reference. If the client hits you with something out of left field, you can say, "That's not what we agreed to do."

Who Sets the Goals?

If you know what you're doing, you should do more than merely participate in the setting of goals. You have to bring your expertise to bear on the situation and lead the client in the right direction. You have to take control of the whole process.

In June of 1984, when basketball star Michael Jordan joined our firm, he spent that summer playing basketball for the U.S. Olympic team. By the time he had returned in September, David Falk, who is a close advisor to Michael, had set up an entire program of goals, objectives, and strategies he felt would benefit Michael. We explained to Michael what these goals were, and he agreed to go along with our ideas.

Our first goal was to mount an endorsement campaign that would establish Michael as an exciting, high-flying sports hero. Along with our major objective, we wanted the contract with a major shoe manufacturer to encompasss several other criteria: We wanted a shoe identified with his name, we wanted a specific advertising commitment for a sports hero campaign, and we wanted the company to assist Michael in supporting one of Michael's favorite charities or scholarship funds.

Nike agreed to our terms, and so the famous "Air Jordan" shoe, which first defined Michael's superstar image, was born. Through that campaign Michael's face became known all across America, even before he played his first pro game, and by the end of the first year, the Air Jordan basketball shoe was one of the top sellers in America.

We set other goals for Michael. We wanted his deals to be long-term endorsements with established major companies. We didn't want hit-and-run, capitalize-on-the-moment deals, which could perhaps overexpose or overcommercialize him.

We wanted Michael, a down-to-earth, warm, regular person, to sign with companies that reflected his own values and lifestyle. Michael, for instance, publicly stated that he loved McDonald's food. That was our entrée to McDonald's. We felt McDonald's wholesome family image was right for Michael, and we liked what they were doing with the Ronald McDonald House. It was the kind of image we wanted Michael to be associated with.

Michael is a sharp dresser and has a model's perfect athletic physique. To enhance this image, we signed him with Bigsby and Kruthers, a fine men's clothing shop in Chicago.

With each new contract, we discussed with Michael exactly what our goals for him were, and how, through the image he presented to the public, he could enhance these goals greatly.

Getting your client on track may be a matter of setting a financial goal: X dollars in new revenues or Y dollars in savings. It may be the completion of an architectural project by a certain date or the sale of a novel to a certain publishing house. Whatever that goal is, it should be declared early and unabashedly. This way, both members of the team—you and your client—will be pointed and moving in the same direction.

Paying Attention

To presume to tell clients what their goals should be places a very high premium on paying attention. You must listen to what the client is actually saying rather than what your *preconceived* notions about what he or she should be saying or what you expect him or her to say.

When we began representing Connie Carpenter Finney, the first American to win a cycling gold medal in the Olympics, our natural assumption was that she would want to maximize her exposure and expertise through opportunities within the cycling world. As it turned out, she was sick of competing, she didn't want to coach, and she didn't want to do a lot of the typical trade endorsements. Connie is very articulate and what she did want to do was become a national spokesperson for her sport.

We got her jobs as a commentator on NBC, USA Network, and on ESPN and writing assignments with *The New York Times* and *Bicycling Magazine*. We also looked for companies that were involved in cycling that would use her as a spokesperson for the sport rather than as a product endorser, and we reached an agreement with Nabisco for this purpose. Since Connie's mother had suffered from multiple sclerosis, we helped Connie become involved in raising money for MS through a program she helped create called MS Bike Tours.

In any client business there is always the danger of coming up with a knee-jerk "that's the way we do it here" solution because you haven't heard what the client has really said. A financial advisor, for instance, is almost never told, "I want my money to grow very slowly." But if he or she is paying attention, and understands the client's desire for security and protection, then the advisor will adjust his or her advice accordingly.

Goals Are Flexible

Goals are made to be changed. As a client's situation changes, his or her goals must change, too. Again, being responsive and paying attention are all-important. Bob Lutz was one of my very first tennis clients in 1970. Ever since I had known him, he had always been an easygoing, happy-go-lucky friend. For years, I wondered if when he retired he would slip into the role of club pro or manager somewhere.

One day in Phoenix toward the end of his active playing career, Lutz turned to me and said, "Donald, I've been having terrible nightmares lately. I dream that I become a club pro somewhere and I do nothing but teach kids and rich ladies how to hit tennis balls all day long. It really terrifies me that once I quit the touring circuit I'm going to be . . . *bored* for the rest of my life."

In this case, our goal became to keep Bob from gravitating into a position as a club teaching pro. What we did was try to expose him to as many nontennis opportunities as we could. We talked about stocks and bonds and decided against it, but Bob did decide to go to real estate school. I'd sought to involve him in other business deals, and wanted to provoke his interest and get him focusing on doing *something*—get his mind off worrying about doing *nothing*. I wanted Bob to know that there was, indeed, life after tennis.

It's worth keeping in mind that your relationship with a client is a journey—a continuum—and what may be appropriate goals for you and the client at the beginning of the relationship may be totally inappropriate as it nears its end.

Agreeing on Ends Means Understanding the Means

If a tennis player's goal is to win Wimbledon or to win a tournament or to get ranked in the top one hundred players, he or she usually knows what that is going to take: a combination of fitness, training, practice, the right schedule, and more practice. To reach goals in "real life" the steps are usually not that clear-cut.

Setting goals sounds great because goals are abstract. Even when they are very specific, they are usually out there in the hazy future. It is the interim steps that make goals real, and clients in all fields of endeavor need to be made aware of the steps and commitments necessary to reach their particular goals.

When tennis player Tim Mayotte came to us, he told us, "Just do my marketing for me." Tim didn't understand what that implied, and unfortunately we didn't explain it to him adequately.

Our public relations department had developed a four-page campaign describing how we were going to make Mayotte better known and more attractive to sponsors. We did a photo shoot, produced a brochure, and did a lot of work. When we presented the campaign to him, he balked. He decided that he didn't want to devote the time we felt was needed to make the campaign work.

Ultimately, we had to compromise. We backed off and did what we could. If we had discussed more thoroughly what we wanted him to do at the outset, perhaps we would have met with more success. At worst, we wouldn't have wasted time devising a plan the client wasn't comfortable with.

A more successful effort centered around Mark Gorski, who was the first American male to win a cycling gold medal in the 1984 Olympics. When Mark came to us, we knew we would be able to get him more income—he had been earning $20,000 a year from all endorsements—but the problem was that even a big piece of the cycling pie was not very large in those days.

Steve Disson, our senior vice president, represented Mark and we both agreed to work together to make the sport of cycling bigger, and that was the deal we struck at the outset: He would teach us about the world of cycling, and we would represent his interests as the biggest American name in the sport. Our interim goal was to expand the economic base of the sport, and with Mark's help we staged the first U.S. vs. U.S.S.R. cycling challenge match and are currently organizing a six-event American Grand Prix of cycling sponsored by the Sundance Company.

These efforts have brought new consumer product companies into cycling who are now beginning to spend significant sums to sponsor athletes and promote them in advertising and public relations. Mark Gorski is now getting a bigger piece of a bigger pie as a result.

Educating the Client

No matter what your field of expertise happens to be, getting along with clients is mostly a matter of educating clients about their own best interests, and yours. For the sake of everyone involved in the relationship, clients need to be made aware of what they can reasonably expect from you (and what they can't) and what they should reasonably expect from themselves.

There never has been a marriage manual that has been 100 percent on the mark; if there were such a book, I wouldn't be writing this one. A *marriage* is what much of a strong client relationship boils down to. When expectations are met, in a marriage or in a client relationship, there is harmony and growth. When expectations are not met, bitterness and a sense of failure follow. What follows are a few suggestions for avoiding that kind of unnecessary defeat in your client relationship.

Protecting Clients from Themselves

Recently, we got a call from one of our tennis clients who said he was too sick to fulfill a doubles exhibition obligation the next day. We knew this particular client well enough to know that he probably just didn't feel like going, and we also knew that if he didn't go, it would be a huge problem for the several major companies sponsoring the event.

For an entire day we bombarded him with phone calls, always with the same message: "You have to go. These people have advertised and promoted this event and without a fourth player, the match falls apart. The other three players are relying on you. You have to do what's right."

Fortunately, he relented and fulfilled his commitment, but unfortunately, this behavior happens all the time in the sports business. Skipping a tournament or not showing up for a sponsor's clinic is not like missing a class in school. There are ramifications that many professional athletes just don't seem to appreciate. So often it seems we are in the business of explaining to many of our clients how the real world works.

The need to educate clients in what otherwise might seem to be perfectly obvious to you is not unique to the sports world. Lawyers often assume their clients know more about the law and how it works than they actually do, which can lead to problems down the road. Advertising agencies also suffer greatly from this same sort of failure. Halfway through a campaign, clients will respond with some non sequitur indicating that they never understood the campaign in the first place. When this happens, it is less the clients' fault than the agency's. The agency, after all, is the expert. It is the agency's responsibility to educate clients about how the agency's expertise is helping the client realize his or her goals.

I will admit that educating professional athletes in the ways of the world (where the concept of "consideration for others" is completely new to some of them) has often been an ongoing education for us as well. One of the toughest clients I ever had to deal with in this regard was Ivan Lendl. The following examples demonstrate our efforts over the years to get Ivan to act in his own best interest.

Ivan is intensely private—almost a loner. Early on, the problem was partially the language barrier. Invariably, Ivan would sit through mandatory press conferences after a match with a scowl on his face and respond to questions with one- or two-word answers. He didn't like being with the press and it showed. The result was a lot of otherwise avoidable negative publicity.

After one such press conference, one of my colleagues, Ray Benton, went up to him and said, "Ivan, if you would just smile, and as you get up to leave, smile again and say, 'Thanks very much,' I will assure you an additional million dollars in endorsement income a year."

Ivan gave him an intense, serious look—as though he was about to tell him off. What he was really doing, though, was considering the "offer." Finally, Lendl shook his head and said, "No . . . it's not worth it."

Eventually, we came to realize that Ivan is one of those people who feels a loss of control if he can't convince himself he already knows more than everyone else in the room. He would accept our advice only after first being given the opportunity to *reject* it.

A few years ago I had breakfast with Ivan right before Wimbledon. The English press had written a half dozen scathing articles about him, really nasty criticism. I had arranged to have this meeting to propose some ways to make him seem a little warmer and friendlier to the media and fans in England.

I said to him, "There are a couple little tricks that will soften your image. If you beat a guy badly, as you go to shake hands, just pat his shoulder with your other hand. Or, if you really don't like the guy, at least look him in the eye, try to smile, and say, 'Nice match.' All the photographers and TV cameras will be on you right at that instant, and those little gestures will do wonders for your image."

Lendl contemplated this for a moment and again indicated that what I was saying was so against his nature that it would take away his competitive edge—sheer nonsense, in my opinion.

Two days later at Wimbledon Ivan slaughtered someone 6–1, 6–2, 6–1. When he went to the net to shake hands, he put his arm around his opponent's shoulder and smiled. I almost fell out of my seat. That was how we had to educate Ivan: First he had to reject the game plan outright, and then we would often see him adopt it later as if it were his own idea. Fine. Any way to get the job done. Ivan's relationship with both the public and the press has improved dramatically over the years. It was the result of a great deal of hard work and persistence—both his and ours.

Protecting Yourself from the Client

Perhaps the major part of educating the client is educating him or her to your own needs and desires and to the parameters of the relationship. A failure to do so ends more client relationships than anything else. If you fail to exercise this control, your time becomes the client's rather than your own, and you end up resenting the client.

It is important to find a way to educate the client toward accommodating you. If approached correctly, clients are usually quite willing to be accommodating, but you have to spell out precisely what the parameters are early in the relationship. The longer you wait, the more difficult or awkward saying much the same thing is going to be down the road.

With the benefit of hindsight, this was probably our problem with Ivan Lendl. When Ivan first came to this country, he was a brilliant young Czechoslovakian tennis prodigy who was naive about the world and unfamiliar with the ways of American culture. Since he was young and America was foreign to him, we made a conscious decision to protect him from all the normal everyday worries. ProServ arranged his plane flights, took care of his practice time, tennis balls, tennis strings, chauffeurs, got him credit cards, and paid his bills. All he had to do was show up and play tennis.

By doing this, Ivan came to feel that this was all part of our job. Before long, if anything ever went wrong in any capacity, it became our fault. If his tennis balls didn't arrive, rather than simply walking twenty feet to buy some on his own, he would call us long distance from overseas and demand, "Where are my tennis balls?" It would have been far better if right from the start we had let him do more for himself, as the other tennis players did. We never set the proper ground rules from the beginning.

Although it is best to get the rules straight up front, things often change. There is no harm in changing the rules as long as you do so with tact, consideration, and some sensitivity as to how the client is going to be affected.

Sara Fornaciari, a senior vice president at ProServ, is one of the highest-level female client managers in sports to my knowledge. When Sara was single, her clients were the most important aspect of her life. As far as she was concerned, there was very little distinction between when she was on duty and when she was off. If clients called her at home at night, she didn't mind. It was part of the job.

Once she got married and had a baby, Sara's situation changed dramatically, and so did some of her rules. One by one, while she was speaking or meeting with her clients she would say, "I have to leave now to get home. If I don't, I might as well not be married." Or she'd make a joke out of it. She'd say, "Please don't call me at home anymore after seven because the baby is sleeping, and if you wake up that baby, I'm going to be so angry you aren't going to want to talk to me anyway."

Since many of her clients were young women athletes, a lot of them hoping to get married and raise a family themselves, they not only observed Sara's new rules, but were very much interested in Sara's progress in terms of learning to *balance* her career and her family life. In some cases it actually strengthened the bond between Sara and her clients.

How to Talk to Clients

Your ability to establish mutually desirable goals, to educate the client, and to get along with the client in general all come down to one thing: how well you are able to *communicate* your wishes and desires to the client.

The main factor in effective client communications, of course, is understanding the approaches that work best with each client. There are a number of communication guidelines that apply across the board when dealing with clients—things to do and things to avoid that will help you get your points across.

- *Kisses of death.* The two things that will kill you in talking to clients are not talking to them at all, or, when you do talk to them, making them feel that the conversation is the least important thing you have to do that day.

Clients can handle bad news a lot better than they can handle no news at all; in fact they accept screwups, missed deadlines—almost anything but *silence.*

If you make a client feel as if he or she is not high enough on your priority list or that your time is more valuable than the client's or that you have more important people to take care of first, he or she is eventually going to sour on the relationship.

When you are talking or meeting with a client, train yourself to focus your entire attention for that moment on the client. If you are distracted or preoccupied with something else, it is better not even to take a phone call or have a meeting, because your voice and manner will reveal that you aren't "all there" for the client. Tell others you will call back later so you can give the matter the attention it needs. It is better to give a client 100 percent of your attention for three minutes than 50 percent of your attention for half an hour.

- *Good news/Bad news.* One of the reasons you want to be sensitive to a client's moods and needs is so that you can anticipate the problems that are most likely to come up and head them off at the pass. Indeed, anticipation is so important that the entire next section deals with this subject. I mention anticipation here, however, because it is so fundamental to effective client communication.

Whenever presenting a client with good or bad news, the two most important questions you need to ask yourself are Is the mood right? and Is the timing right?

Though there is never a good time for bad news, it is worth keeping in mind the philosophy behind those good news/bad news jokes. Try to soften the bad news by delivering it along with some good news.

If there is no good news to deliver, create some. There's usually some small silver lining someplace.

Delivering good news to a client takes as much forethought and calculation as bad news. I will often have a good deal to present to a client, but I know that if the timing is "wrong," right after a tennis client has won a big match, for instance, the response is probably going to be "I'm worth more." Generally, if the client has just lost, the last thing he or she will want to discuss is business, no matter how big the offer.

The best strategy is to wait until the client is relaxed, and in a receptive frame of mind. It also doesn't hurt to "presell" good news: "I've got some interesting news for you, but now is not the time to discuss it. Let's talk later this afternoon."

• *Use disclaimers.* One communication technique I have come to use quite naturally is the use of disclaimers. Whenever I am about to offer criticism or advice I will open with, "I may not know much about this, but . . ." Or "I could be wrong, but . . ." Or "I'm not an expert on the subject, but . . ."

This strategy lets the listener know that you are inviting discussion, and that you are not trying to cram anything down the client's throat.

• *Be conspiratorial.* Another technique, not only for communicating with clients but for building trust and confidence, is to be conspiratorial. Often, when negotiating on behalf of a client, we will prearrange with the client the roles we are to play—good guy, bad guy routine—whatever. Not only are these little scenarios very effective in sales situations, they have the dual effect of including the client in the team effort.

• *Give them a choice, but limit the menu.* What frustrates most people who represent clients is that they work like crazy to get a deal done and then the client, upon being presented with the deal, immediately second guesses them.

It's frustrating and often disheartening, but if you put yourself in the client's shoes, you can see that always to be told what the deal is—always to have the terms dictated to you—isn't an enviable position to be in. The natural response for the client is to try to participate in his or her own deal. To avoid these potentially unpleasant situations, you have to be willing to use some applied psychology. If you say to your young son, "It's time for your bath," he will probably argue. But if you say, "Do you want to take a bath now or take a bath in a half hour from now?" the youngster is forced into making a decision.

Sometimes with clients, however, you simply have to resort to the other old parent standby, the "Because I said so" technique. Often, for instance, we will tell a client, "We got X dollars for an endorsement," and even though this figure might represent six months of negotiations, the client will respond by saying, "Why don't you go back and try to get X plus Y?"

Rather than give a blow-by-blow description of the negotiations, I will simply say, "Look, we need to decide on this offer right away: A) you can take the deal, or B) you can turn down the deal, but there's no C." It's my way of letting the client know that this is the culmination of all my effort, and there isn't another penny to be squeezed out of the deal. It's amazing, when presented this way, how often "A" wins out.

● *Don't ask; tell.* There are certain situations, such as matters of integrity or self-destructive behavior, when you can't give the client a choice. On a couple of occasions, when I strongly suspected one of our athletes had a drug problem, I have refused to give the client any money above the monthly allowance, once even under the threat of a lawsuit.

Fortunately, this isn't the type of situation that most people who represent clients have to deal with. What most of us have to deal with is those clients whose basic nature is to resist. With these clients you don't ask, you tell.

As always, it comes back to knowing your client—knowing which ones respond best to a direct statement, or to general coaxing, or to making a choice in the matter.

When I was negotiating with the San Antonio Spurs for Duke guard Johnny Dawkins, the Spurs owner insisted that we get him to rookie camp without a signed contract. I knew this was an ego thing with the owner so I recommended to Johnny that he go. Dawkins, who is a very smart player, refused. The common tenet is that you don't go to rookie camp without a signed contract, and that was the advice given to him by practically everybody, including his father.

At that point I had met Johnny Dawkins only twice in my life. I didn't know how hard to push him, so I picked up the phone and called his coach at Duke, Mike Krzyzewski. I explained the situation and Krzyzewski said, "Listen, Donald. You don't ask Johnny Dawkins if he wants to go to camp. You tell him. In fact, give me an hour, and I'll tell him."

An hour later the phone rang. It was Krzyzewski. "Johnny will be in camp. Just tell him what plane to be on."

From that point on I knew how I had to communicate with Dawkins until we earned his trust and confidence.

They Have to Know You Mean It

It is the nature of some clients to take as much as they can get. So when you put your foot down, when you say "No," or "This is the way it has to be," or "Here's the deal, and that's final," they have to know you mean it.

When I first met Bob Lutz he was a nineteen-year-old student at

USC, and I was the U.S. Davis Cup team captain. One time in order to get him out of school early for a Davis Cup match, I proposed to his professor that I monitor one of Lutz's final exams. Incredibly, the professor agreed to go along with this arrangement.

On the morning of the exam I showed up in Bob's room with the test. "It is now one minute to nine," I said. "This exam will begin promptly at nine A.M. and you will have exactly three hours to complete it." I looked at my watch and sixty seconds later I said, "The exam has now begun."

When I checked back in at eleven, Lutzie was frantically writing away. He said, "Donald, there is no way I can finish by noon. I've got to have a little more time."

"This exam will end at twelve noon on the dot," I repeated, "whether you're finished or not." He said, "I'll fail, and I won't be able to play Davis Cup against Australia." "Be quiet, Lutzie," I replied, "and keep writing."

At the stroke of twelve I ended the exam. It turned out that Lutz passed okay. He was one of those guys who was always testing the limits. You had to let him know that you meant what you said. From then on Bob knew I didn't make idle threats.

Knowing Your Own Weaknesses

To communicate effectively with clients, you also have to factor in your own weaknesses. If you tend to be dogmatic, or have trouble expressing your real feelings, or sometimes speak too hastily, then these can be a major hindrance to your ability to communicate effectively with your clients. Usually, the most you can do about it is to take appropriate precautions and to be self-aware. As for me, I am a very emotional person. Sometimes I can be too aggressive, or I fly off the handle too easily. Since I know this about myself, I am very quick to apologize to clients and very quick to admit when I am wrong. A healthy dose of self-awareness doesn't hurt client relations across the board.

Anticipation

We once represented a real estate promoter who had put up the lion's share of sponsor's money for a successful tennis tournament we had organized for him. The finals had been telecast on PBS. At his party that evening, the sponsor had set up a giant TV screen to rerun the finals.

At the end of the show as the credits rolled, and our client was receiving plaudits from his guests, the PBS announcer came on and said, "This program was made possible by grants from the following companies: Transamerica, Paine Webber, Seiko . . ." and named a couple more.

As our client watched this, he went white. He didn't understand that these companies were PBS television underwriters, not sponsors of the tournament. He mistakenly thought we had sold the tournament twice, once to him and once to these other advertising companies. He stood up and muttered, "I know when I've been screwed," and stormed out of the room. Like that, the party was over—and so were we.

Knowing how much our client's ego had been involved in this tournament, we should have anticipated this possibility and explained to him beforehand the difference between sponsoring a tennis tournament and underwriting costs for a PBS production, which involves receiving credits at the end of the show.

Anticipation is so important, and anticipating correctly can produce such positive results.

When recruiting Notre Dame basketball star Collis Jones years ago, it became obvious to us that his parents, particularly his mother, felt that Collis had not received the amount of publicity he should have had at Notre Dame. This insight prompted us to have the Hilton Hotel in Dallas put up a "Welcome Collis Jones" sign on their large outdoor marquee the day Collis and his parents were there for the contract signing ceremony. This thrilled Mrs. Jones, even more than the six-figure contract we negotiated for her son that day.

In thinking about our proposal to Seiko, and asking them to become the official timing device of the Grand Prix tennis circuit, we were almost certain they would bring up the fact that Wimbledon had a permanent Rolex clock mounted near the center court scoreboard. As we anticipated, this was one of their first objections to the deal.

Because we had anticipated correctly, we were able to show them that in spite of the Rolex presence at Wimbledon, Seiko could become the dominant name in tennis timing. We were ready with the names and dates of ninety Grand Prix tournaments where the Seiko timers would be used on court, and most important, the amount of television exposure available to Seiko over the year. Because we anticipated we were able to begin a long-term, multimillion-dollar relationship with Seiko.

Anticipation—I can't think of a client business where this doesn't apply—is also what resolves 90 percent of client problems at the outset.

David Falk and I were recently in Chicago negotiating Michael Jordan's new contract with the Chicago Bulls. That evening the three of us had dinner together to discuss our progress. We were hesitant to tell Michael what our final numbers were since the negotiations were still going on (and rather badly) but he demanded to know. We were about to tell him when Charles Oakley, Jordan's teammate and good friend on the Bulls, walked into the restaurant with his girl-friend, spotted us in the back, and came over to our table.

Oakley was talking, goofing around, showing off a bit, and out of

the corner of my eye I could see that Michael was starting to get
irritated. After about ten minutes of this, Michael stood up and said,
"I have to go," and walked out.

Later, on the way back to our hotel, I said to David, "We have
to call Michael right away. He left angry. He was irritated that
Oakley interrupted our conversation, and he's going to hold us re-
sponsible."

David called and asked Michael if he was upset. "Yeah," he said.
"I got tired of listening to Oakley talk and I wanted to continue our
conversation. I wanted to know what the numbers were."

It was important that we had responded to Michael's irritation,
because that irritation is exactly the sort of reaction, if not anticipated and headed off at the pass, that can fester and become a
problem. If Michael had slept on that frustration overnight, his
feelings would have intensified by morning. By the time we could
have gotten together again, our good negotiating efforts might have
been secondary to his feelings.

I wish there were some other way to say it, but so much of
anticipating a client's actions and taking the appropriate measures
goes back to knowing your client. As I mentioned earlier, Bob Lutz
was always one of those clients who was testing the limits—seeing
what he could get away with. But as long as we knew this about him,
we could always take the appropriate countermeasures.

One year, Lutz was due to make a teaching appearance at a local
summer tennis camp. Weeks before he began his litany as to why he
wouldn't be able to make it: his wife was going into the hospital, a
relative was sick, his dog was having puppies.

As I well knew, Lutz simply hated to do clinics. He'd say, "Why
do I have to stand out there with two hundred kids telling them,
'Watch the ball, bend your knees?' "

The day before Lutz was due to appear at this camp he called me from Milwaukee. "Donald," he said, "I'm here at the Milwaukee airport and . . ."

"Hold on for a minute, Bob," I said, "I have another call." I put Lutz on hold and called my travel agent on the other phone and got a schedule of all the flights out of the Milwaukee airport for the rest of the afternoon to Madison, Wisconsin, where the camp was located. Then I got back on with Lutz. "Sorry, Bob," I said. "Now what were you saying?"

"Donald," he said, "I can't make that camp appearance tomorrow. There are no flights available from out of here to Madison."

"Bob," I said, "I just booked you on Air Wisconsin," and I told him the flight number and the time. "But you have to hurry," I added. "Your flight leaves in twenty minutes."

"Aw, hell," Lutz said. "Why did you do that?" I said, "Because I know you so well, Lutzie. I knew you'd come up with some excuse, but I thought you might be more creative!"

● *Get on the plane and go.* There's a tremendous advantage to discussing any problem or potential conflict face to face as opposed to over the phone. We have a rule around the office: If you think you have a problem with a client and if you remotely suspect it's best handled in person, don't second guess yourself. Get on a plane and go. That, as much as anything, describes our corporate style. It shows the clients we care. The main benefit is that the two of you can sit there and discuss the problem face to face, which greatly relieves the potential for further misunderstanding.

This approach also works as a preventive measure. A well-timed meeting or lunch date can prevent hours of doubt and speculation, all unnecessary and completely avoidable.

● *Disclose all conflicts.* In addition to representing tennis players, we also manage tennis tournaments, arrange for their television coverage, sell sponsorships, and occasionally I will provide color commentary on TV. As a result, the charges of "conflict of interest" aren't new to us. But I know to anticipate this accusation and how to respond to it—immediately and directly.

For me, the key to mitigating the conflicts problem is to make *full disclosure* of our various roles to all of our clients—individuals, corporations, and other interested third parties. As long as our involvement is fully disclosed to all parties up front, I think much of the criticism about conflicts is unjustified. If ProServ can create more job opportunities for our clients by organizing tennis tournaments and sporting events, our clients all benefit as a result. As long as we disclose any conflicts at the beginning, any client has the opportunity to say, "Count me out."

There are, of course, some occasions in many service professions (particularly law, finance, and sports) where conflict of interest is so pervasive that your role is disabling. In these cases, of course, you must explain to the client why you feel a conflict of interest is a problem and excuse yourself. It should also be your responsibility to recommend a surrogate service provider when the conflict-of-interest circumstance arises and you must withdraw.

● *Watch for out-of-character behavior.* Although every client is different, all usually tend to act in character. When certain clients whine and complain or talk about being injured, sick, or hurt, we respond, "Sure, we're sorry," and leave it at that. But if a client who never whines or complains is upset about something, you better really pay attention. You can anticipate that something important is wrong, and it pays to find out what it is.

● *Watch out for in-character behavior.* By the same token, clients can also be amazingly predictable. What you discover to be the client's Achilles' heel will mostly remain the client's Achilles' heel for as long as you represent him or her, barring some miracle. I can

remember the one brief, shining moment when we convinced ourselves to represent the clown prince of tennis, Ilie Nastase. Off the
tennis court, Nasty is a warm, funny, charming, decent guy, but he
is also a bit of a flake. Fortunately, we more or less knew what we
were getting ourselves into and were able to anticipate and deal with
some of his flakier maneuvers.

One time Nastase entered himself into two tennis tournaments the
same week, figuring, I suppose, that he couldn't possibly reach the
finals in both tournaments.

One of the tournaments had been an official event, for which we
had him scheduled. He had booked himself in the other event as an
exhibition. The two tournaments were only a hundred miles apart.
I guess he figured he could pick up some extra money with a little
juggling of playing schedules.

It worked like a charm through the earlier rounds, but of course,
Nastase managed to reach the finals in both tournaments.

We now had the unenviable task of having to inform the unofficial
tournament that Nastase was not going to show up for their finals.
Naturally, the tournament director went berserk and demanded to
speak to Nastase directly. Nasty apologized sheepishly but said that
eleven o'clock the next morning a limo was going to pick him up at
his hotel and take him to the other tournament, and that's all there
was to it.

Fortunately, someone from ProServ overheard this conversation.
It dawned on him that it would never occur to Nastase to make sure
he was getting into the right limo. He would just get into whatever
limo showed up, and play wherever he was let out.

The next day a ProServ person was waiting with Nastase, and sure
enough, at five to eleven, a limo drove up—the "wrong" limo, sent,
of course, by the promoter of the unofficial tournament.

There is absolutely no doubt in my mind that if we hadn't been
standing there with him, Nastase would have driven off, no questions

asked, and the promoter of the nonofficial tournament would have felt like one smart guy.

Tricks of the Trade

There is an artifice as well as an art to representing clients. Over the years I have discovered there are certain tricks of the trade or stratagems based on a simple understanding of human nature which tend to aid and abet the client relationship.

Let the Client Run the Show

Clients like to know the representative is working for them, and no one likes to feel they are being controlled by their agent.

Sometimes it's good to let the client control the meeting—ask all the questions, get his or her points across. Don't feel shy about asking the client for advice in his or her area of expertise. Not everyone can benefit from a better jump shot, but, over the years I have found our clients to be a great source of knowledge and expertise on a whole range of subjects.

My brother, Dick, for instance, took Spanish lessons so he could communicate better with our Spanish-speaking clients and their families. Dick relates especially well to Argentina's Gabriela Sabatini, because she appreciated the effort he was making to become bilingual. Dick encouraged Gabriela to help him with his Spanish, and her expertise gave her the chance to be the mentor in the relationship, bringing them closer together as a result.

"Why Did You Leave?"

What I have found over and over again is that it pays to find out why the client left his previous relationship. If it was a sin of commission, don't repeat it; if it was a sin of omission make sure that item is number one on your priority list.

Before Jimmy Connors came to ProServ, he was represented by one of our competitors who had gotten him a slew of exhibition matches but very few long-term endorsement deals. He was thirty at the time and asking himself, "What will I have when I retire?"

It didn't take an Einstein to figure out that Jimmy would judge our performance largely on how effective we were in bringing in the long-term (four years or more) blue-chip endorsements, and that's where we have concentrated our efforts.

If You Can't Solve It, Find Someone Who Can—Fast

As you become a trusted advisor, your clients will often turn to you for help with problems which are outside your field of expertise. Clients shouldn't expect you to be all-knowing. You should be willing and able to try to help them get the kind of advice and counsel they might need in other areas, whether it is taxes, investments, medical, legal, psychological counseling, or real estate. Keep a file of up-to-date, high-quality references. Everything you do to enhance your role as a problem solver strengthens and deepens your clients' trust in you.

How to Separate the Wheat from the Chaff—Quickly

Stan Smith was not only one of my first clients, he is also one of the best people I've ever known—almost to a fault. Early in his career, it became apparent that Stan never wanted to disappoint anyone. He was always calling us to say he had just met someone on a plane who had a promising business proposition and to ask us to follow up on it.

We always tried to reach the people whom Stan had met, with very few concrete proposals resulting. Stan thought we were not taking these requests seriously and eventually became somewhat irritated at what he perceived to be our lack of follow-up on real opportunities. Here was one of our most important clients, and he was feeling we were not taking him seriously enough.

After giving this a lot of thought, I proposed the following solution: We would follow up on every lead that Stan gave us, but first we would ask everyone to put their proposals in writing. "If they are serious," I said, "they won't mind. And if they aren't willing to take the time to put their business or investment propositions in writing, then they probably would not have been the type of business partner you'd want to have anyway."

Not only was Stan satisfied, it eliminated the 90 percent chaff from the 10 percent wheat, and we didn't feel like we were wasting our time or going through the motions.

This solution not only solved the problem of separating the wheat from the chaff, it also was the fairest approach to the client. He knew we were taking his requests seriously and were following up where appropriate.

Rules of the Road

In seeking to understand the client relationship and to build a client business based on that understanding, there are certain lessons I doubt I could have learned any way other than through hard knocks and experience. The following are four of the most important:

Rules Are Made to Be Flexible

Rules exist for the mutual benefit of you and your client. One of the things that can drive a client absolutely berserk are rules, policies, or procedures that, even though they may be set up for perfectly valid reasons, end up taking on the character of immutable laws. People with guard dog mentalities should not represent clients. A client's needs don't always fit neatly into your rules and regulations, and there is nothing more infuriating than to be told, "I'm sorry, that's our company's policy and there are no exceptions."

Adrian Dantley's mother once came by the office to pick up a check from his account. When she was told it was not ready because we had not yet been able to reach Adrian to get his "approval" to write her the check, she threatened to have Adrian resign as a client right then and there.

For an organization such as ours, which has to deal every day with ex-wives, current girlfriends, and future business partners, this is a perfectly valid precaution and one we take as a matter of course. But Adrian's client manager had to learn the hard way that Adrian and his mother were *both* clients of the firm. This was one of those times the rules were in need of some bending.

Rules Are Made to Be Changed

If enough clients object to the same rule, policy, or procedure, don't fight it; either modify it or change it. When we first got into basketball representation, we billed our time on an hourly basis and charged our clients for expenses, as a law firm. A number of clients objected to this procedure; they did not understand why their fee was one amount for one month and a different amount the next, and we were spending half our time with our clients justifying our billing procedures rather than generating income for them. So we changed. From that point on we gave the clients a choice. The basketball clients could either continue on an hourly rate or pay us a straight percentage, whichever they preferred.

You Don't Always Have to Get Your Way

When I first started to represent clients, I used to think that I always had to get my way with the client in order to give him or her the best representation. Somehow I felt I knew what was in the client's best interest more than he or she did, which is often dangerous.

I have learned that you don't have to get your way 100 percent of the time. As a manager I have to remind myself continually that it's the client's life and that a client doesn't like to be told what to do all the time.

You should also use compromises as currency, as "debt" to be repaid. When something important comes along, you can then say, "I agreed on that one. Now let's try it differently this time."

Never Violate a Client's Goodwill Even When It Goes Against Your Own Best Interest

Trust and confidence is a two-way street. If a client places trust and confidence in you and if, for whatever reason, you betray that trust and confidence, the ramifications are usually disastrous.

Most of the time, the client's and your interests are exactly the same. There are those occasions when they can come into conflict, and when that happens, you must always put your client's interest before your own.

When we represented Tracy Austin, her parents very much wanted us to hire her brother, Jeff, to work at ProServ. Jeff had gone to UCLA law school and had been a tennis player on the circuit, but I knew that there was a risk in hiring him to work for us—in teaching him the business firsthand.

It was almost a no-win situation for us to hire Jeff. If it didn't work out, that would damage our relationship with Tracy and her parents. If it did work out, we ran the risk of Jeff's leaving and losing one of our biggest clients (Tracy) to her brother. Knowing full well the risk we were taking, we decided to hire Jeff anyway. It was in keeping with the spirit of our relationship with the entire Austin family, and not to do so would have created other serious problems with Tracy.

As it turned out, Jeff had a real knack for the business, and as we feared, he later left ProServ and took his sister's business with him. Still, if I had to do it over again, I would probably make the same "mistake" again. It was the right thing to do at that time for the Austin relationship, even if it wasn't necessarily the right thing to do for ProServ.

If you look at your own business, I'm sure you'll see repeated instances where the client's wishes are antithetical to yours—and deadly to the life of the relationship as a whole. After a point, there's nothing—truly nothing—you can do about it. The real pros know this and know that the best course of action is to shrug a shoulder and move on to the next item on the agenda.

CHAPTER FIVE

GETTING
THE JOB DONE

A common myth created by the media is that most professional athletes earn millions of dollars from endorsements and other commercial activities. In truth, only a handful have the celebrity status and charisma to command national endorsement deals and even among this handful, there are only about a dozen superstars from any sports era—a Nicklaus and Palmer in golf, a Connors and Ashe in tennis, or a Jordan and Bird in basketball—who can literally name their price and pick their deals.

As a rule, most athletes earn far less from off-the-field business activities than the public believes. Yet the myth is so pervasive that many pro athletes themselves are stunned to learn the truth. On any number of occasions we have taken on clients who can't understand why they aren't swimming in a pool of endorsement deals immediately. Ironically, our job, in a way, is to perpetuate the myth by doing everything we can to make our clients the exceptions to the rule, rather than the examples of it.

As I said earlier, you earn the client's respect, first and foremost, through *performance.* This can mean different things to different people. In most client businesses, "getting the job done" ultimately comes down to the bottom line, either directly (such as with agents or brokers) or indirectly (such as with consultants and advertising firms). You can give a client the best advice in the world, and he or she may even take it, but at the end of the day it is salesmanship and results that make your relationship with your client succeed.

Persistence

So much has been written about the value of and need for persistence in all aspects of business I can hardly add anything worthwhile— other than the idea perhaps that the more you appreciate the competitive aspects of selling, the easier it is to appreciate why persistence is the key to winning.

When tennis legend Rod Laver was once asked the secret to his success, he said, "I just keep bashing the ball over the net until it's time to go up and shake hands." This sort of persistence was not only the key to Laver's extraordinary success, it is, in fact, the underlying ethic to all athletic competition—the idea of never giving up; the belief that "it ain't over 'til it's over" or "until the fat lady sings." It is what enables football, basketball, and hockey teams to give their best up to the final buzzer even when there is no hope of winning. The only real difference is the terminology: In business it's called persistence; in sports it's called "guts."

When I have a front door slammed in my face, there is nothing I love more than the challenge of coming back at it through the side door or in the backdoor or down the chimney—whatever it takes. If I can turn a deal around with a "What about this . . . ?" or a "Suppose we did that . . . ?" it is often more satisfying to me than a "yes" right out of the box.

Persistence is the groundwork that getting the job done for the client is based on. When persistence is combined with emotion, it leads to a kind of indomitability, best illustrated by the way Jimmy Connors now approaches a tennis match. When Jimmy was younger he was more likely to annihilate opponents—simply blast them off the court. As he has gotten older, it is now more of a steamroller effect. He starts out slowly and deliberately and picks up momentum as he goes along until he is a tidal wave by the final set.

I approach my business deals in much the same way. Sometimes even to my detriment, I become an irresistible force looking for immovable objects to steamroll over. That is the price of admission I've learned to pay. It is far better to be too persistent—to push too hard—on behalf of your clients than to risk losing the deal for not having been persistent enough.

More Than Money

During our first negotiation for Boomer Esiason of the Cincinnati Bengals, I said to Boomer as we began to get close to reaching a deal, "We're only twenty-five thousand dollars apart. We may get all of it, we may get none of it, but most likely we'll compromise. But I'd like your permission right now to try to finalize this thing."

Boomer hesitated, then said, "Can't we push a little harder? Twenty-five thousand is a lot of money. Remember you guys make a commission on that."

"Look Boomer," I said, "let me explain something to you. We've been negotiating this deal for two months now. It's been hardball.

If you think that this is just a matter of making another phone call or that our fee on twenty-five thousand dollars is going to motivate us any more than we already are, then you don't really understand us very well. We want to get every penny of the twenty-five thousand dollars—out of pride. We want to feel we delivered the best possible contract for you, that we rolled up our sleeves and did our job well."

We ended up getting all the $25,000. And I tell this story to other players, because sometimes there is a perception in this business that we're in it strictly for the money, but it's much more than that.

Doing the best job possible is what is really important. As we enjoy more and more success, everybody wants to outshine us, and we want to outshine ourselves as well. We've arrived at the point where the real challenge becomes doing even better than we thought we could. Money—fees and commission—is just a way of keeping score.

Creative Positioning

Not only do you owe your clients your best efforts, you also owe them your best thinking.

Getting the job done for clients is not too different from getting clients in the first place. Much of what applies to recruiting clients and selling them on your services often applies to selling on their behalf. Not the least of these skills is making the best use of the facts available in order to position the client creatively in the marketplace.

The secret of creative positioning is opening up your mind to all possibilities. If you look at something from just one perspective, your mind gets "locked in" and it becomes more difficult to consider all the possibilities. There is a brain teaser represented here that illustrates this. The challenge is to connect all nine dots with just four lines without raising your pencil from the paper.

•   •   •

•   •   •

•   •   •

Give up? The secret is that you have to extend your thinking—and your lines—beyond the dots in order to do it. The difficulty that most people have in solving this is that they limit their thinking to the space circumscribed by the dots. For the solution, see facing page.

Solving problems in the business world also often involves solutions that are out of the ordinary. You constantly have to say to yourself, "Consider the unusual, even the outrageous. Go beyond the conventional borders." That's how some of the best creative thinking happens.

In the book where this puzzle appeared, the author reported that he has subsequently received many other correct solutions, including one from a clever fellow who drew enormous dots and connected them with three lines and from someone else who drew big dots, wadded up the paper and stuck his pencil through it, connecting all the dots with "one line."

How does this apply to clients? Creative positioning involves understanding your client's most marketable and attractive attributes, then opening your mind up to all the possibilities that their attributes might suggest.

This is not, by the way, the stuff of alchemy. You can't make the client into something he or she is not. But you do want to position the facts to present the client in the best possible light.

The solution:

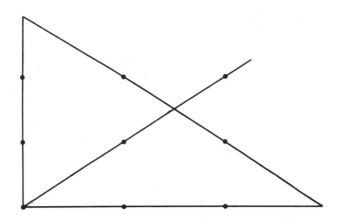

Back in 1983 we signed a woman Australian tennis pro by the name of Elizabeth Sayers. She was the second-ranked player in Australia, but not very well known in the rest of the world.

Although Liz had limited recognition as a tennis player, she had a lot of other things going for her. She was outgoing, very attractive, personable, and articulate, and America was just beginning its love affair with Australia. We decided to position her first as a personable, attractive Australian "export" and second as a promising new star.

We brought her in for a complete beauty makeover and a half-day session with a fashion photographer. At about the same time, she and Cathy Jordan won the women's doubles at Wimbledon. As a result of attendant media coverage, Liz's popularity increased dramatically, and she became one of the most sought-after women players for corporate tennis clinics and events. Her attractive appearance, her warm personality, and her engaging Australian accent were just the right combination.

By correctly repositioning the "facts" about Liz, we were able to enhance her marketability and generate an additional $250,000 in income for her from exhibition appearances and contracts.

It's very easy to say after the fact, "Well, that was obvious," but that's the whole trick to creative positioning.

As it happened, Liz's success helped to alter the entire way in which women's tennis is promoted. Up to that point, the idea was to promote women's tennis as being "just as good as the men's," though people would see the game wasn't played at the same pace. With the success of the Liz Sayers campaign, the U.S. Women's International Tennis Association (WITA) began pushing a more glamorous image—that these were attractive, young, graceful athletes out there—a pleasure to watch for more reasons than the quality of their tennis. That year, in fact, WITA came out with its first women's tennis calendar, showing the players in glamorous attire. Since then a new edition has been launched every year at the U.S. Open, with great fanfare.

Another example of creative positioning involved Stan Smith. During and in the aftermath of Stan's "golden year" in 1972, we were certainly able to make several lucrative endorsement deals for him. However, as the tour victories eventually became fewer and further apart, new deals became harder to make and the old deals harder to renew for Stan.

Later Bob Briner and I were in Landersheim, France, at the headquarters of Adidas negotiating with the master, Horst Dassler. Horst began reciting to us a litany related to the lack of success Stan was having on the court. It was obvious Adidas did not want to renew some of their expensive endorsement relationships with him.

As Horst paused for breath, Bob began to talk about Ted Williams and the classic relationship Sears had with him long after his playing career was over. I saw where Bob was heading and chipped in with a recitation about Joe DiMaggio and the famous Mr. Coffee campaign in the States.

Instead of trying to refute what Horst was saying about Stan's lack of current success on the court, we began to position Stan in such a way as to make his wins and losses irrelevant. We convinced Horst that Stan Smith was the kind of player and the kind of personality whose name would be valuable to a company long after his playing days were over. We renewed all of Stan's deals with Adidas that day.

It pays to be creative and to pursue an alternate approach when your primary one is blocked.

Of course, you may not be in the business of positioning a client directly, but you should always keep in mind the image a client wants or ought to want. An architect who reads "traditional" into the trappings of a client's office might be missing the fact that the client is due or ready for a change. By the same token, a lawyer who is advocating this or that issue must know how strong he or she should come on and whether the client is best served by a hard-edged image or something softer. These choices, made consciously, give an edge to the kind of service you offer the client and help you to stand out from the competition.

Target Your Audience

An image is created in the eye of the beholder. You can have the greatest image in the world, but if you don't get it out in front of the target audience you want to convey that image to, it's all just a waste of time. As a result, you have to do two things with an image: You have to create it, and then you have to find ways to disseminate that image to the key groups that matter.

When we signed Jimmy Connors, one of our aims was to get him better known in the corporate and financial communities. Paine Webber gave us that chance. They signed Jimmy for a series of TV commercials, the first of which was actually to be shot on the floor of the New York Stock Exchange. The director of the commercial was Bob Giraldi, who had also directed most of those wonderful

Miller Lite beer commercials. In other words, we felt there were enough "angles" to attract press coverage.

We sent out a press release aimed at the business community, followed it up with some phone calls, and as a result, *Business Week* sent a writer down to cover the shoot and ran a full-page feature in the magazine on the making of the Connors/Paine Webber commercial. We could not have hoped for better. *Business Week* was ideally aimed at our target audience: the corporate movers and shakers who make the decisions as to how to spend their promotion dollars.

Selling the Client

As I mentioned earlier, creatively positioning the client works in much the same way as when you are recruiting clients: You sell yourself to the client by using the facts about yourself and your organization to your best possible advantage. Naturally, the same approach applies when selling your client to others.

A couple of years ago, we were trying to entice Seiko into sponsoring a challenge match between Ivan Lendl and Pat Cash in Hong Kong. Seiko initially turned us down because Cash and Lendl was not their idea of a dream matchup; at the time Cash wasn't even ranked in the top ten.

Our job, then, was to reposition the facts in order to make the match seem more attractive and exciting. We brought to their attention the fact that Cash had recently beaten Boris Becker, a world-class player, and gotten to the finals in a major tournament. We also told them, "Tennis fans remember the Lendl-Cash final match at Wimbledon," though in fact that final had been something of a disappointment. Just by recalling that match I was able to conjure up the Wimbledon mystique. After some further haggling, we were able to agree on the deal.

Obviously, if making deals for clients were always that simple then anyone would be crazy to be in any other business. This little back-and-forth with Seiko does illustrate a key point about sales: Selling of any kind requires—and handsomely rewards—the ability to think quickly on one's feet.

Getting to Know Them—Quickly

In many sales situations you do not have the luxury of a long-term courtship as you might when recruiting clients. You have to get to know your customers very quickly and make snap decisions based on what you can learn in a short period of time.

I used to think that the most effective selling was, "Have I got a client for you!" I would go into a meeting and immediately I would start to sell, sell, sell! The only problem was that I wasn't closing that many deals.

If there is one lesson I have finally learned over time, it's the importance in most sales situations of talking less, listening more, and asking intelligent questions. *Less* here is always *more.*

There was a time when I might have begun a sales pitch by saying, "I want to sell you a tournament in Orlando," and then would talk about twenty minutes, only to have the other party say, "We're not interested in tennis tournaments in Orlando because our entire business is in Portland, Oregon."

Now I am more likely to start off asking, "What is your core business? What are you looking for in sports promotion? What do you need to know about us? How do you think we might help you?" and so on. I will start to sell only after I have done a certain amount of intelligence gathering.

In selling situations you really do have to shut up and ask the right questions. It's not easy, particularly for the "born" salespeople who are naturally gregarious. It is something you have to be consciously aware of and work on all the time.

Even today, I will sometimes go into a meeting and get really excited about what's been discussed, and off I'll go. As a result, I will miss all but the most obvious of signals.

I once met with Michael Fuchs, the chairman of Home Box Office, to sell him on a musical show we were representing. After a few minutes, Fuchs, who is a friend, interrupted me and said, "I have to tell you something, Donald. I hate musicals. I would never put one on television. Our original programming needs are drama and sports."

Fortunately, Fuchs knew me well enough to stop me from running on at the mouth. If he had been someone else, I might have pitched him for twenty minutes, then he would have said, "Thanks a lot," and I never would have heard from him again.

Don't Feel Obligated to Reveal Your Ignorance

There is that old adage about it being better to be thought a fool than to open your mouth and remove all doubt. Even so, any of us can have a bad day.

I can remember a meeting about ten years ago when we were trying to sell a series of European clay court tennis events to PBS, the public television network. I was well into my pitch when one of the PBS executives cut me off by saying, "We couldn't possibly do this deal. The cost of televising from Europe would be prohibitive."

Satellite technology was relatively new at the time, and in my defense I must say I wasn't involved in our day-to-day television operations. I responded to this executive by putting on my best know-it-all face and saying, "You're absolutely wrong about the cost. With these 'spoons' we can bring in the whole package from Europe for a lot less than you'd imagine."

Everyone in the room, including my colleagues, started looking quizzically at each other with, "What-in-the-world-is-he-talking-about?" expressions on their faces. Finally, one of my associates said somewhat sheepishly, "I think what Donald means is dishes—satellite *dishes*—not spoons."

Here I was, this supposed television expert, and I was rattling on about spoons. It was a classic case of trying to come across as knowing more than I actually knew—and getting caught at it.

Though these PBS executives knew me well enough that they didn't hold it against me, it was the kind of mistake you only have to make once to learn an unforgettable lesson in the limits of "winging it."

Thinking on Your Feet—Quickly

Talking less, listening more, and asking the right questions also gives you a chance to think on your feet and shift gears when necessary—which is most of the time.

The most extreme experience I have ever had in this regard occurred several years back after an associate had asked me, on the spur of the moment, to attend a meeting he had set up with the president of McGregor. We hadn't had a chance to talk beforehand. When I arrived for the meeting, I naturally assumed I was there to meet with the head of McGregor Sporting Goods about possible endorsements for some of our up-and-coming athletes.

I was all prepared to go into my speech, but as we began talking, I sensed that something wasn't quite right. This man seemed to know more about fragrances than he did about sporting goods! Immediately I reverted to my tactic of asking questions: "What do you do? Tell me more about your business?"—anything to buy some breathing room and time to think. He was a little put off at first, but once he got talking, he was very informative—on the subject of skin lotions and perfumes. Turned out the fellow was the president of McGregor cosmetics and fragrances!

When I learned what I needed to know, I switched gears, and I began to tell him about our hottest young female client, Gabriela Sabatini. Three months later we closed a cosmetic deal for Sabatini with this company.

Not all of our turnaround deals are, thankfully, that dramatic. If they were—and if they occurred frequently enough—we'd obviously be doing something else fundamentally wrong. But if most deals begin with a "no thanks," as I believe they do, then your ability to turn them around will depend almost entirely on your ability to think on your feet—to pick up on the subtle nuance or oddball fact, assimilate this immediately into your thinking, then shift gears accordingly and come back without missing a beat.

A Shot in the Dark

Although the specific reasons for talking less and listening more may be to gather information, to give yourself time to think, or simply to avoid putting your foot in your mouth, the overall desired effect is one of control—over the sales environment and the person to whom you are selling. In most business situations, the person who has learned more about the other and revealed less about him or herself will have a subtle yet distinct advantage over the other party, whether it's a matter of learning how best to position your client or product in terms of the buyer's desires, or figuring out just how far the other party can be pushed.

I became agonizingly aware of the need to control the sales environment from one particular situation in which I was totally bereft of even the pretext of control. Admittedly, it was under exotic circumstances.

Several years ago the sheik of Dubai had contacted ProServ through an intermediary because he wanted to create a tennis tournament in his sheikdom. We flew to this small Arab emirate to negotiate with him. Our plane landed first in Saudi Arabia. During our stopover, we learned firsthand about the recent assassination of King Faisal. Apparently a nephew of the king had walked right into the tent where the king held court and shot him dead with a pistol.

With this in mind, my partner Bob Briner and I flew to Dubai to meet with the reigning sheik. We met in a big long tent out in the desert. Sitting around the tent were men toting rifles with falcons on their arms and bandoliers across their chests. We felt very much like we were in a James Bond movie.

As the sheik sat in his tent, his subjects came before him to ask favors or have him settle disputes. As we sat there quietly watching this procession, we tried, of course, to conceal our awe over the whole scene. We had never negotiated with a sheik before and we wanted to appear cool, detached, and not like a couple of bumpkins or tourists from the States.

Finally, one of the sheik's minions approached us and said, "The sheik will see you now. Please follow me." We were led into a separate private meeting room behind the sheik's throne and had been waiting there about five minutes, feeling terribly on edge, when suddenly we heard a loud bang.

Thinking the noise was a shot, I dived for the floor and tried to crawl under a couch, which must have been all of about twelve inches off the ground! Briner, who is a very big guy, shrank into a fetal position. We both thought we were goners.

When we looked up, there was the sheik standing over us with his arms folded and an amused look on his face. He attempted to make us feel less like idiots by saying, "I'm sorry for the shock, but that was merely a light bulb that exploded." He was very polite but couldn't hide his amusement. Throughout the remainder of the talks and even through the final negotiations, it was difficult for us to "hang tough" on any issues without feeling a little foolish. We knew that the sheik knew that when the going got tough I would head for cover and Briner would head back for the womb!

Hidden Agendas

No matter how good you may be at picking up subtle signals or reading between the lines, you must take what you learn with a grain of salt. In many sales situations in which you don't know the other party very well, there are often hidden agendas that you cannot possibly perceive. Indeed, one hidden agenda cost us a major deal for Tracy Austin.

We had spent four months negotiating with the Wilson Sporting Goods Company trying to conclude a racquet deal for Tracy, who had just won the U.S. Open at age sixteen. Two of our people had even spent several days with Wilson in Chicago trying to finalize the contract terms but without much luck. Finally, Dick Calley, the president of Wilson Sporting Goods at that time, called to say that he and his general counsel were flying into Washington on the company jet to meet with me personally. "I want to wrap this thing up," he said, "even if it takes all weekend."

The next morning, the Saturday before Easter, we met in my office with Calley and Wilson's counsel Pam Nada. It was a very tough, unpleasant negotiation, and Calley's counsel was making it a lot more unpleasant than necessary. It was almost as though she were trying to sabotage the deal.

The final crucial issue came down to whether Tracy's name would be on the racquet face itself or on a hangtag attached to the racquet. We had insisted that the name be on the racquet itself. Though Calley fought me on this point, he relented in the end.

Finally, we had agreed to all terms—the dollars, years, royalty, territory, and so forth. Calley said to his counsel, "Pam, why don't you and Tracy's lawyers go into the conference room and work out the final language?"

After they left, we sat in my office making small talk. While waiting for the others to finalize the language, we heard louder and louder voices coming from the adjoining conference room. It was Wilson's general counsel, who came running out yelling, "Dick, they are trying to change the deal." She was still insisting that Tracy's name be on the hangtag, not on the racquet face.

I was furious. We had made a deal, and she was now reneging. I said, "Dick, you have to control her. She is changing the deal and is very emotional about it."

Suddenly she burst into tears. "Also, they are being mean to me," Pam said, "and unfair to Wilson."

At that point Dick Calley totally overreacted. He turned to me and said, "That's it, forget the whole thing. The deal's off." Then turning to his counsel, he said, "Pam, dear, let's get out of here." They stormed out, the deal in shambles.

I was dumbfounded. As I stood there, I thought to myself: "Four months of negotiation down the drain." It made no sense whatsoever for this to happen over a resolvable issue.

Six weeks later I learned that the president of Wilson and his general counsel had both resigned and run off together to Mexico to get married! That's one hidden agenda I had totally missed—she was the boss!

The Art of Negotiating

Twenty years ago the author John McPhee wrote a classic book about tennis called *Levels of the Game,* a title which referred not only to the levels of skill that separate one class of player from the next, but also to the many psychological levels—all the mental games— that go on during a match.

For me, nothing in business more closely parallels the psychological gamesmanship of competitive sports than negotiating. Perhaps because of my professional athletic background, nothing sets my competitive juices flowing faster than knowing I am about to go into a tough, important negotiation.

Whether I am negotiating for a client, for ProServ, or for myself, I find the nuances of the process—the gamesmanship involved—endlessly fascinating.

Donald Trump, for instance, has said that his constant courting of the media is just another negotiating practice: the bigger the "Trump" name becomes, the bigger percentage of deals his partners or adversaries *expect* him to get.

In my case, I have been accused, on occasion, of being less interested in the negotiating process than in merely getting my way—like a spoiled child who must be placated. This is what so intrigues me about the gamesmanship: If that's what an NBA owner must tell himself in order to justify paying more than he wanted for a player, that's fine with me. In the "inner game" of negotiating, his feeling that we don't "play nicely" becomes another weapon in our arsenal.

There is, however, one significant way in which gamesmanship in negotiating does differ from gamesmanship in sports. In sports there are two opposing general philosophies—the "winning is everything" faction at one end of the spectrum and the "it's not whether you win or lose but how you play the game" faction at the other.

But in negotiations, winning or losing is determined by *how you play the game.*

It's All in the Preparation

I think having been a trial lawyer has helped me as a negotiator in any number of ways, but nothing so much as learning to appreciate that if you enter the courtroom properly prepared, the trial itself is that much easier.

Trials are won or lost in the preparation stage, and so are negotiations. Getting all your ducks in a row and preparing yourself for any eventuality is what wins negotiations, not tricks, artifice, or bluster. I believe so strongly in adequate preparation that when my colleague, David Falk, and I were preparing to negotiate Patrick Ewing's contract with the New York Knicks, we actually conducted several mock negotiation sessions in which we took turns playing Knicks management, each trying to top the other in coming up with the tough questions we thought we'd be asked.

In preparing for a negotiation, what are the kinds of things you should be looking for? First, you need all of the pertinent facts at your fingertips, all the facts, not just the ones that are easy to get.

The good attorney goes into a courtroom fully prepared. He or she knows everything there is to know about the witnesses and what questions to ask. The one thing that can turn around an otherwise winnable trial is the surprise fact or unanticipated answer from a witness. We have one rule around the office whenever anyone is briefing someone else for a meeting: no surprises.

Surprises can also kill you in a negotiation. Many times we will only know 90 percent of the story, and it turns out that the missing element is the one thing that jumps up and bites us later on. As a general rule, the most important facts in a negotiation are the ones known only to the other party, such as their absolute top dollar limit. They are certainly not obligated to reveal to you what you want to know. So you must deduce the facts that you don't know from the facts that you do know. It is the known facts that flush out the unknown facts. The more facts you have at your fingertips going in, the more you are naturally going to pick up along the way.

I can remember negotiating my very first basketball contract for Collis Jones in 1972. The owner of the Milwaukee Bucks said to me, "Our highest club salary is one hundred and fifteen thousand dollars." I said, "I don't believe you." He said, "I'll show you all my contracts."

He showed me three or four contracts, all of which were for under

$115,000 a year. What I didn't know at that time (which I certainly have learned, of course) is that annual salary alone for a team sport athlete doesn't mean that much. You have to ask: How much money is deferred? What about loans and other forms of compensation? Is there a signing bonus? What are the incentive playing bonuses? The reporting bonuses? and so on down the list.

The only "defense" against this sort of ignorance is knowledge and experience—knowing the facts. Today, with the help of the players' association, we know what every basketball player is paid and how the compensation packages have been structured. There is a great *power of precedent* in any negotiation. If you know every salary in the league, you know almost as much as the owners do. Now we never have to guess about salaries anymore.

We also must know the facts that will justify our asking prices. What we try to do is take our figures out of the realm of subjective measurement of the athlete's talent and into a level of more objective criteria such as the player's value to the team and his or her name draw in bringing fans into the arena. In team sports, we have practically become economists in certain negotiations.

Becoming the equivalent of an "economist" in your area—a master of the facts, whatever they are—is crucial to your success. Although you might be concerned with banking or design or law or advertising, there is a body of specific information that could make you or break you.

For us, it's the difficult task of determining one man or woman's commercial worth. With an athlete such as a Michael Jordan, we will factor in his value to the franchise if Chicago Bulls owner Jerry Reinsdorf decides to sell the team. Additionally, Michael puts fans in the seats, brings PR value and excitement to the city of Chicago, allows the Bulls to raise ticket prices, and even lets them make better arena and concession deals for themselves. All these economic factors must be figured in to justify the player's value to and impact on the team—and therefore his or her real worth in that situation.

Though a client's value and impact is one way to measure a fair price, we must also rely on experience and instinct to determine what something is worth. I call it having a real "sense of the market"—the X factor. It's the same when an expert in real estate looks at a piece of property and says, "That's worth five hundred dollars an acre rather than one thousand dollars an acre." The expert is bringing all of his or her prior knowledge to bear on determining the value of that particular real estate. Anyone who represents clients in any field should have some sort of sense of his or her client's intrinsic market value. If the representative doesn't, he or she probably doesn't have the right "feel" for the business anyway.

Before going into any negotiation involving money, you also need to know all the factors relating to the size of the pot. No business can operate indefinitely at a loss. Whether that business is IBM or an NBA franchise, it can't afford to pay its employees more than it takes in in revenues.

Yet pro basketball owners, many of whom made their millions in some other business, were such profligate spenders that, in 1983, in order to protect themselves from themselves, they negotiated a player's salary cap with the NBA players' association. The problem is, the formula by which the cap is determined is so complicated that almost no one understands it or can figure it out—especially the owners. As a result, the salary cap has had the ironic effect of giving us an edge in basketball negotiations.

David Falk, in our office, has an almost photographic memory of the salary cap of every NBA team. Since the salary cap was instituted, I doubt that we have had a player negotiation during which the owner hasn't said, usually as their first line of defense, "We can't do that because of the salary cap."

David will respond, "But if you trade so-and-so, as you plan to, then you can make the cap work." This puts us at a great advantage because the owners immediately know that we know as much (or even more) about their ultimate maneuverability under the salary cap rules as they do.

You also need to know the size of the pot because there is definitely such a thing as a "Pyrrhic" negotiating victory, which occurs when you get your price, but you so severely handicap the other party, he or she either can't or won't want to deal with you again. If we are negotiating with a local tennis promoter who is putting on a one-night exhibition, we can't very well insist on an extra 10 percent if his profit margin is so slim that it makes his whole effort a break-even or loss proposition.

We want to make sure he makes money, because if he does, he will call us in six months or in a year to promote another event. If he loses money, we may never hear from him again. He'll be out of business, and we'll be chasing a debt we are never going to collect.

Sowing Some Seeds

Once you know all the facts you can possibly know, there are opportunities to put some of these facts to work even before you get down to the real nitty-gritty of negotiation.

Many years ago, when I was negotiating one of my first basketball contracts with Sam Shulman, then the owner of the Seattle Supersonics, I discovered that Sam also owned a chain of indoor tennis clubs throughout the Midwest. Before I went out to see him, I called up one of his tennis managers, whom I had known from my tennis days, and asked him what Sam was doing in tennis.

"The person who loves tennis," this guy said, "isn't Sam, but his wife. She is nutty about the game." Since the Shulmans lived in Beverly Hills, where Jack Kramer had his home, I asked if the Shulmans knew Kramer. "Not personally," he said, "but I know that Mrs. Shulman is crazy about Kramer."

On my way to meet with Mr. Shulman, I called Jack and said,

"You're coming in as my consultant to negotiate this basketball contract." Jack said, "What the hell are you talking about? I don't know the first thing about basketball." I said, "I know that. Just come with me and let me do the talking."

As Sam and I were working out the details of the basketball contract, his wife was pacing around the house, impatiently waiting for us to get done with our negotiations, so she could meet Kramer.

Sam sensed her impatience, which put pressure on him to get on with the business. After about two hours, he had basically given us what we had originally asked for.

Afterward Shulman said to me, "You really are a rogue, Donald. I bet you knew my wife is crazy about tennis. But what you couldn't have known is that she grew up playing with a Jack Kramer tennis racquet, and absolutely idolizes him."

"Oh really?" I said.

To use your known facts to "seed" a forthcoming negotiation obviously demands a certain amount of *anticipation.*

The year we represented UCLA basketball star Marques Johnson, we were fairly certain he would be drafted number three by the Milwaukee Bucks, who that year also held the number-one draft choice. That presented a problem for us because everyone knew that Indiana all-American Kent Benson would be drafted number one that year. Why was that a problem? Because Benson's agent wasn't very experienced and also had formerly worked for the Bucks organization, we were afraid that Benson was going to end up with a low contract. If they drafted Marques, they would expect him to accept an even lesser contract at the number-three position in the NBA draft.

To head off the trouble I was expecting, I called the Bucks owner, Jim Fitzgerald, the day *before* the draft. "Please don't draft Marques Johnson tomorrow," I said.

"Why?" he asked. I explained, "Please don't draft Marques Johnson because he's the best player in the draft, even though he won't go until the third or fourth pick. And I'm telling you right now that he's going to cost more money than Kent Benson because he's a much better player. If you choose to draft him, understand that we're going to demand more money than you are going to end up paying Benson. So what I'm suggesting is that if you're not prepared to do that, don't waste your number-three draft choice on Johnson."

With that call I was in a win/win position. If Milwaukee did draft Marques, I had the perfect argument: "I told you we were going to demand more than Benson got." If they didn't draft him, then we would go to Chicago, who needed him more than Milwaukee needed him anyway.

As it turned out, the Bucks drafted Marques. Sure enough, as we began negotiating, they trotted out Benson's contract to convince me. I pushed it back unread and when we set our price, Fitzgerald said, "That's crazy. How can you expect us to pay Johnson more than the very first player selected in the NBA draft?" I said, "I told you last week I was going to ask for more than you had to pay Benson."

Ultimately, four months later, he agreed to our price.

Cutting Off the **Thems** and **Theys**

The oldest negotiating trick in the world—so old, in fact, that it isn't even a trick anymore—is to go through the entire negotiating process and then have the other party say, "This looks fine, but now I've got to get the final okay from my president." The ploy is to come back and say apologetically, "My boss wouldn't accept these figures. I'm afraid we'll have to work out an agreement at a lower dollar amount."

One of the facts you need to know before going into a negotiation is who the ultimate decision maker is going to be and whether the person with whom you are negotiating has the authority to bind his organization. You need to cut off the "thems and theys."

If you suspect the other side will pull the old "I-have-to-check-this-out-with-the-boss" routine, you should spell it out at the outset: "I want to deal with the decision maker. If you're not the decision maker, let me talk to the right person. Who do I negotiate with—you or someone else?"

Actually the client manager has a very subtle advantage in that with rare exception he or she *cannot* bind the client. The knack is to keep the other party from having the same "out."

Several years ago we represented North Carolina basketball star Phil Ford in a negotiation with the Kansas City Kings. After a long, tough negotiation, we had finally reached the point of crossing all the *t*'s and dotting the *i*'s when Kansas City general manager Joe Axelson said to me, "Now let me get the final approval from the owner."

"Don't give me that 'talk to the boss' nonsense, Joe," I said.

"But you have to go back to your client to get his approval, don't you?" Joe replied.

"I'll tell you what," I said. "If Phil doesn't go along with our recommendation, I will resign as his lawyer. But," I added, "I assume you'll resign as GM if you recommend this to your owner and he refuses to approve it."

"That's not fair," Axelson said. "The difference is that you have a lot of clients and I only have one job."

He was right, of course, but I got my point across, and as it turned out, we ended up making the agreed-to deal.

A top New York entertainment lawyer we respect by the name of Mike Rudell has a routine he uses to cut off the thems and theys. In his bookcase in his office sits a stuffed toy monkey, and whenever he's in a negotiation in which someone starts to pull the "I'll have to get back to you on that" routine, he might respond to the next point by saying, "I'm sorry. I'll have to check that out with my monkey." Or he might say, "I'm sorry, but my monkey says he's not going to let me do that." Rudell doesn't have a them or a they, so he uses his monkey. And the monkey usually cuts off the other thems and theys very quickly by making the other guy feel a little silly and not his own man.

Naming Numbers

As negotiating has become an increasingly popular business subject, I have read and heard over and over again that the actual amount of money involved in a negotiation is only *one* of the crucial items that needs discussion and may indeed not even be among the most important items.

As a general rule, this is absolute hogwash! Obviously, any negotiation involves more than money. That's why agreements can often be thirty pages long rather than three pages or why negotiations can go on several months or even years rather than hours or days.

Most negotiated terms emanate from the size of the dollars. Paradoxically, I would bet in almost any business that the contracts with the biggest numbers attached to them are also the contracts with the best terms across the board and the most favorable language. This observation belies the conventional wisdom that negotiation is a process of trading off.

When it comes right down to it, there are really only two ways to negotiate numbers. Ninety percent of negotiations come down to a game of highball/lowball: You name this number, I name that number, and we end up somewhere in between. This to me is a lazy man's, ineffective way to negotiate.

The other way is to come in with your ducks in a row, set your price based upon justifiable facts, and stay there. Over the years we have had success in doing the latter, based largely on sound preparation—and knowledge of the market—and coming in armed with a set of advantageous facts.

We may ask a large sum of money in some negotiations for our clients, but it will never be a number out of touch with reality, either for the player or for the marketplace. The offer will always be one that we can justify, not just to the other party, but in our own minds as well. When we explain why we think an athlete is worth X dollars, the club we're negotiating with may say, "I don't like your offer," but they can rarely say, "I think your offer is off the wall."

As anyone who has ever negotiated knows, if you're planning to name your number and stick to it, being able to justify your offer with tangible facts may get you, under ideal circumstances, as far as first base.

What we try to do is get all the way home. What we have done successfully in the past is to establish a *presence,* a palpable sense that we aren't kidding, that we *mean* what we *say.* If you choose to negotiate this way, there are no tricks, but there are certain rules and guidelines that you are best advised to follow.

- *You must be able to walk away.* The first rule of negotiation, any kind of negotiation, is that you have to be able to walk away from the table. You have to know before you sit down that you can say, "No, I'm not going to accept that." If you get into a situation where you *must* make a deal, it severely limits your ability to make the deal you want because you yourself know at the end of the day you can't pack up and walk away. Everything then becomes a bluff, and you never want to be in a situation where you are having to bluff your way through a negotiation.

There are times when I have been too reckless, when I've walked away from deals that maybe we should have done. But that might be the price you have to pay to get your clients what they deserve the other 95 percent of the time.

• *Use the power of precedent.* Let's say the other side offers $300,000 and you offer $800,000, and they say, "Can we compromise at six hundred thousand?" and you say, "No, we're going to be at eight hundred thousand four months from now because that's what we think the deal is worth." If you can then refer to five other negotiations in which you didn't budge from your number, your position carries more weight when it comes time for them to decide whether you are serious or not.

The power of precedent and presence is one of the real values of having someone with experience represent you in any sort of negotiation. The representative can point to his or her track record, even if it's in a different field or sport.

• *When to make the first offer.* The first offer from the other side is no more than a piece of information, and it can tell you volumes. Here's why: If our figure going into a negotiation is a million dollars a year, but the other side opens with an offer of $900,000, right away we know we may not be asking enough. If their opening offer is $200,000, that tells us that this is going to be a long, tough negotiation.

You force the other side to name their price first, not to be disagreeable, but because you want to know what their opening number is, which gives you a significant edge in the negotiations.

I remember when I was out in California to negotiate for basketball player Kermit Washington with Pete Newell, then the general manager of the Los Angeles Lakers. Pete, a soft-spoken, nice man, said, "Donald, what do you want for Kermit?"

"First," I replied, "I'd like to hear what you have in mind. You know what your salary structure is." Pete said, "My instructions from Jack Kent Cooke are that I don't make the first offer."

There was silence. Neither Pete nor I said a word for about three minutes. It seemed like three years. At the end of that time Pete started laughing, and said, "I see we're at a stalemate." I said, "No, it's just that no one's talking." Pete responded, "You're really serious. You're not going to make the first offer, are you?" I said, "No, not today, not tomorrow, not ever. The Lakers are the ones who drafted Kermit, not me."

After enough time went by, he finally believed me.

Pete knew that he would have to make the first offer if the negotiations were to get off the ground, and finally he did in our next meeting.

The one exception to having the other side go first would be if you suspect that their offer will be so low that you want to get yours on the table first. The idea is to "shame" the other side and discourage them from making such an "embarrassingly low" first offer.

Recently, as we began renegotiating Michael Jordan's contract with Chicago Bulls owner Jerry Reinsdorf, my instincts were to make the first offer for precisely that reason. We suspected Reinsdorf's offer was going to be absurdly low. When we arrived, I saw that Reinsdorf had already prepared a typed written offer sheet, and my curiosity got the better of me. As copies of the offer sheet were being passed around the table, I could see that the key number was $6 million for four years—light years away from what we had in mind.

Realizing I had made a tactical mistake, I quickly, if rather clumsily, said to Reinsdorf before his paper reached me, "Just to get things started I can tell you we're looking at a thirty-nine-million-dollar package for Michael for ten years and want to make sure we have the opportunity sometime today to explain how we arrived at that figure."

Reinsdorf looked at me in stunned silence. "There seems to be a gap," he finally said. By this time I had been handed his written offer sheet. "No, Jerry," I said, "there seems to be a chasm."

If I had been smarter or less curious, I would not have had to resort to this little ploy and would have come on strong with our opening position first. Then the chances are Jerry might not have shown me his offer sheet at all, but would have opened with something more realistic and closer to what we were seeking.

Ultimately, Michael re-signed with the Bulls for an eight-year contract totaling monies far closer to our first offer than to theirs.

Make Them Believe You

In order for a statement such as, "I'm not going to make an offer, not today, not tomorrow, not ever" to be effective, the other side has to believe that you are serious. That is the essence of naming your number and getting it. Your credibility is on the line.

In many negotiations, there comes a *moment of truth*. There is a point where you come together and you say, "We're going to do X, and we're not going to do any more." They reply, "We're going to pay Y, and we're not going to pay more." The fundamental task is for me to know whether they mean it. Or for them to know whether we mean it.

When I say, "Our player is worth eight hundred thousand dollars, that's his market value, and here's why it's his market value, and we're not budging. Either pay the eight hundred thousand dollars or he's sitting out," the other side has to know that I'm dead serious, or else my client is going to end up with a lot less money.

One time, after a particularly long, vitriolic, and fruitless negotiation with one NBA team, we were at a stalemate, when we received information convincing us that the NBA had taken steps to pressure the rival American Basketball Association's Denver franchise from making a fair offer for our client's services. We decided we had a pretty good antitrust case.

So I called Larry O'Brien, the NBA commissioner, told him what we were thinking about doing, and set up a meeting. Before we met, I hired an outstanding antitrust law firm in Washington, Williams & Connolly, to prepare a thirty-five-page antitrust complaint against the entire league.

When I went to see Larry I handed him this document. "Here is our complaint," I said. "We haven't filed it yet, and we don't want to file it. But if you don't force the league to do what's right—to match Denver's offer—we are going to file it exactly a week from today."

O'Brien, who had known me from our Kennedy campaign days, believed me. He got all the other league owners to ante up five to ten thousand dollars per team to offset the difference between what the NBA club had offered to our client and what Denver had been prepared to offer. The NBA knew we had a strong case against them, and they knew I meant it when I said I would file suit against them if they didn't do what was right by our client.

● *Understand and use leverage.* Leverage, or which side needs the deal more, is central to any negotiation and the price you are eventually going to get. The key is recognizing the leverage you have and not being afraid to use it.

Both professional basketball and football, for instance, instituted the player draft system to prevent bidding wars among the owners. What they failed to consider is that as a result, they are virtually obligated to sign their first draft choice. If they fail to do so, this sends an awful message to the fans and ticket holders and the advertisers who support the team locally. Appreciating the value of a first-round draft choice is what I mean by recognizing leverage when you have it.

Sometimes it is impossible to gauge the leverage you may have until the negotiation is well underway. Jimmy Connors once received an offer from Kellogg's which wanted to use his name in a Corn

Flakes commercial. Jimmy uses the product, and the commercial didn't involve any of his time, but the fee they were willing to offer was so low, we respectfully declined.

Almost immediately they came back and doubled their offer. Now I was curious. That told me we had some leverage we didn't initially realize we had. As it turned out, the commercial was going to name superstar athletes who actually *ate* Kellogg's Corn Flakes. They could not very well sign up a middle-level tennis player without defeating the whole idea behind the campaign. They wanted Connors: They needed Connors.

We turned them down again, and again they doubled their offer. At this point we kept saying no until they finally balked. Thereafter we ended up with ten times the original offer.

● *Outlast them—and don't negotiate with Lamar Hunt.* It often comes down to this, and the one advantage I find I have in negotiating is that I am extremely determined and sometimes a little stubborn.

What happens when both sides are equally stubborn? As the coach of Notre Dame once said, when asked what happens when Notre Dame plays Holy Cross and both teams pray in the locker room for victory, "Sit back and watch one hell of a ball game."

A number of years ago I was engaged in a marathon negotiating session in Washington, D.C., with Lamar Hunt, founder of the WCT Tennis Circuit and owner of the Kansas City Chiefs football team. The negotiations had gone on all day and had proceeded well into the night. It became obvious that Lamar was trying to outlast me in a battle of wills, and I was simply not going to give in. As the evening wore on, I found myself bordering on fatigue and incoherence.

At one point I excused myself to go to the bathroom, but my real mission was to splash cold water on my face to try to revive myself. When I returned to my office, I found Lamar on the floor doing push-ups!

I never did find out whether Lamar was exercising to keep himself alert, or to convey the impression that he felt like a tiger. Either way, I must say that from that point on I felt like I was negotiating with Superman.

When Opportunity Knocks . . .

Other than being well prepared and having all your facts and figures at your fingertips, perhaps nothing is more fundamental to successful negotiating than knowing how to be opportunistic. What is opportunism? It is two things really. First, it is knowing how best to use any leverage you have going into a negotiation in a practical way. Second, like the good trial lawyer (or, as I mentioned earlier, a good salesperson), it is knowing how to take advantage of the informational crumbs that may inadvertently be tossed your way during the negotiation itself.

During our negotiation for Johnny Dawkins with the San Antonio Spurs, which I mentioned before, we were getting nowhere because Spurs owner Angelo Drossos was insisting that Johnny come to rookie camp, even though he was unsigned. I argued against this, but then Angelo said, "Tell you what. If you get Dawkins to camp, I promise you I'll make a fair market offer for his services, after he's in camp."

Drossos unknowingly had given me an opportunity. He was a man with a big ego who liked to dictate rather than negotiate, but I knew he was also a man of his word. I believed that I could take that phrase—"fair market offer"—and nail Drossos to the wall with it. In effect, he had agreed to give me whatever we could justify as fair.

I got Johnny to come to rookie camp a week later, and as I sat in the stands with Angelo watching the Spurs rookies playing the Dallas Mavericks rookies, Johnny Dawkins absolutely stole the show. Every time he scored a basket, I would say to Angelo, "That's another ten thousand dollars, Angelo."

That night, when we got down to serious negotiation, I just kept saying over and over again, "Angelo, you promised us fair market value." As a result, from an opening offer of an average of $110,000 per year for three years, we got Johnny a four-year contract calling for an average salary of $420,000 per year.

In terms of having one opportunity after another simply handed to us, the most extraordinary negotiation in which I have ever been personally involved was with the New York Knicks for the services of Patrick Ewing.

My partner David Falk had spent a lot of time thinking about what to ask for Patrick. I remember him walking into my office with a yellow pad and showing me what he had written: "Opening offer: $30 million/10 years." At that time the highest-paid player in the NBA was making $2 million, the highest-paid rookie was making $1.2 million per year. I looked at David and said, "What did you have for lunch? You must be off your rocker." He replied, "You really have to understand that this is an unusual situation. We really have some unique leverage here."

Was he ever right!

First, in a nationally televised lottery, the Knicks, who were desperately in need of a winning team, won the rights to the first draft pick, which everyone knew would be Patrick, who had been touted for almost two years as the "savior" for any team lucky enough to draft him. Sure enough, the Knicks selected Ewing first, and already we knew we were in the catbird seat.

Next we were the beneficiaries of a most extraordinary request. The draft took place in early May, but the actual negotiations could not begin until after the regular season ended on June 18. But shortly after the draft in May, the Knicks called and asked, "Do you mind if we put Patrick's picture on our season ticket brochure?"

"By all means," I said. "Be our guests." I couldn't believe it. Now the Knicks were virtually locked into signing Patrick. If they didn't, they could have had real problems with the N.Y. Consumer Protection Agency, because now they had sold $5 million worth of new season tickets using Ewing's picture on the cover of their brochure!

During this time we picked up some additional leverage. We signed Patrick to a contract with Adidas for well over a million dollars in guarantees. Now we could wait out the Knicks indefinitely.

In fact, at one point in the negotiations, I said to the Knicks, "What's the worst thing that could happen to Patrick if we don't reach an agreement? The worst thing is that he makes a million dollars this year from Adidas, he goes back into the draft, and a different team drafts him next year." When I said that, they became apoplectic.

That's how we stood when formal negotiations began seven weeks later. Right away, the Knicks threw out what Akeem Olajuwon, the number-one draft choice from the previous year, was making.

"Olajuwon is the highest-paid rookie in history," they said, "and we'll do ten percent better. Look, here's his contract."

I took the contract without reading it and handed it back. (A favorite ploy.) "We're not talking about Olajuwon," I said. "We're talking about Patrick Ewing." I knew they were in a position where they simply could not walk away, and I wanted to make sure that *they knew* that we knew that.

If New York doesn't make the deal, they get killed in the press: They get laughed out of town, they lose their first draft choice, and they have potential lawsuits from paying ticket buyers.

We continued to negotiate for three months with the Knicks management team headed by Jack Krumpe and Dave DeBusschere. Suddenly, in September, I got a phone call from Arthur Barron, a senior vice president of Gulf & Western, the Knicks' parent company. He said, "Donald, can you come over and talk to me this afternoon? I want to discuss Patrick's insurance situation."

When we went to see Mr. Barron, he announced in the first ten

minutes that he had his personal jet waiting to take him to Paris at
4:30 that afternoon. That was not a big deal to me because I assumed
he was simply trying to impress us, but when he got up and excused
himself ostensibly to take a phone call, it occurred to me that Barron
was going to make us an offer for the entire deal right now. I thought
to myself, "This is incredible. We have been negotiating with both
Krumpe and DeBusschere, New York's basketball experts, for over
four months, and now in a few minutes, their boss is about to make
a new offer on his own."

Sure enough, Barron came back in about ten minutes and announced, "I would like to wrap this whole thing up right now." He
made us an offer, and it was a damn good offer, too—above where
we had been stalled for months with Krumpe and DeBusschere.
After being handed an opportunity like this one, I simply could not
resist. I countered Barron's offer by increasing our previous position
by 10 percent, rather than seeking to narrow the gap even further.
When you are talking in millions of dollars, 10 percent more is a big
number.

It was 3:30 P.M., and we were at that critical moment of truth in
this negotiation, and Barron had to leave for Paris shortly. He had
already told us that. In doing so, he handed us another opportunity.
I sat there thinking, "We are in no hurry. He wants to close the deal,
leave for Paris, and be a hero to all of his people. All we have to do
is sit here and keep saying, 'Sorry, but this is the best we can offer.'"

We finally closed the deal around 5:30 P.M., with a contract worth
well over $30 million in cash, which is still the largest amount in the
history of team sports contracts today. I felt elated for Patrick, but
almost sorry for Krumpe and DeBusschere, whose authority and
expertise had been totally undermined. I called Krumpe at home the
next morning and stated, "Jack, I hope you understand that Barron
called me."

"I'm not sorry you upped your offer," he responded. "Maybe they
will learn something from it in the long run."

The Art of the Middleman

A large portion of client business consists of personal representation—using your expertise on behalf of an individual. That you must always act in your client's best interest is a given, but what those best interests are can sometimes be a matter of conjecture.

In order to represent your clients most effectively, you must also be cognizant and sensitive to the needs of the person to whom those interests are being represented. That is the art of being a middleman, the person charged with making the deal happen, but making it a deal that leaves both parties satisfied. Situation ethics comes into play; your judgment must constantly stand up to your own personal sense of what is right.

As a lawyer in a criminal case, the ethics are very clear; you do everything short of breaking the law to try to get your client off. But after the trial is over, the client does not then become partners with the prosecution. When you're representing a client in the sports business, that is exactly what happens. Often your client has to live in harmony with the "enemy" on the other side of the bargaining table once a deal is done.

This is one of the reasons we rarely tell our team sport clients what the clubs originally offered for their services. We don't want the client to hold a grudge against his prospective employer, if he would be upset or disappointed by it.

Most of the time, though, these "playing God" decisions are not so clear-cut. One time an advertising agency with whom we had done a lot of business had inadvertently used a photograph of Ivan Lendl in a print ad without permission or paying the normal fees. When we brought this to their attention, the agency said, "You're right. We did it. How can we settle this?" Here was our dilemma. On the one hand we had an obligation to Lendl to negotiate just as hard on his behalf as if this were a "clean deal." On the other hand, if we, in essence, forced the company into paying an unreasonably large fee, we would be earning their eternal enmity for Lendl.

Complicating the picture even further: Where did our own self-interest lie? If we did not have an ongoing relationship with this agency, would we be as likely to be agreeable? Having to answer these sort of questions isn't always fun. It helps to have certain guiding principles you can apply to these middleman situations.

In ProServ's case, we want to make a deal that we refer to as "the high end of fair." In other words, we want to get as much as we reasonably can for our client, but we also want to make a deal that is ultimately fair for both sides.

Sometimes I will say to one of our young guys, "You did a great job, but the company can't afford it. You made too good a deal for your client."

Even if the company is foolish enough to make the deal, it will come back to haunt you. They will get out of it legally or illegally at their first opportunity, and that will be the end of your relationship with that company. Part of knowing how to use leverage is knowing how *not* to overuse it. The other side knows when you have ramrodded a deal down their throats to meet a specific revenue objective for a client, and they will resent you for it. You may have won the battle, but you will have surely lost the war.

The better strategy is to get what you need out of the deal and to allow the other side to get what it needs out of the deal. Be fair and reasonable. That way, you will do business over and over again. Most often, the best deals are the fairest ones for both sides.

Which brings us back to the Lendl example above. What did we do? We settled for $40,000. The agency didn't feel like we had taken advantage of them and because we were paying attention to our client's interests, Lendl ended up with some easy money. When Lendl asked us where the money had come from, we said, "An ad agency inadvertently used your picture, and they're paying you forty thousand dollars for their mistake."

The Price You Sometimes Have to Pay

The one caveat to the preceding advice is that if you have to err, you must always err on the side of your client. Anyone who is going to be successful in the personal service business must accept up front that during the course of your business life, there are times when you are going to lose certain relationships if you are consistently serving your clients' best interests.

When we represented the television rights to the French Open, we had had a contract with CBS for three years, and at the end of the contract and their thirty-day exclusive negotiating period, we learned that NBC was planning to offer us more money than CBS.

Feeling an obligation to CBS, I went to Neal Pilson, the president of CBS Sports, and asked him to increase their offer. "I'm not here to negotiate," I said. "I'm telling you that unless you raise your offer by at least one hundred thousand dollars, you're going to lose the French Open." Pilson thought about it for a couple of minutes, but it was obvious he didn't believe me. He felt I was bluffing. He said he'd think about it and get back to me.

Instead, Pilson's boss at CBS went behind our backs directly to our client, Philippe Chatrier in Paris, the head of the French Tennis Federation, and tried to undermine us. He visited Chatrier and asked, "Do you trust Donald Dell? Do you think ProServ is doing a good job for the French Open?"

When Philippe told me about this, I was furious, and whatever obligation I felt we had to CBS immediately evaporated. We presented the NBC offer to Chatrier, and he accepted it shortly thereafter.

Before CBS had learned about the NBC deal, however, Pilson called to apologize for CBS's behavior. Now desperate to keep the French Open, he said to me, "I know you're angry, Donald, and you have every right to be, but please don't screw me on this one."

I felt terrible. Here was the head of CBS Sports asking me not to "screw" him on this deal, when in reality CBS had already lost the event two days earlier.

We, in turn, lost CBS's goodwill in the process. CBS took the news badly. It took three years for their wounds to heal, before CBS felt comfortable to deal with us again. It's not as if there are countless TV networks out there. I have to admit that negotiation hurt us, but if I had to do it over again, I probably would do the same thing. If CBS had wanted the French Open as badly as they said, then they should have been willing to pay for it and shown more respect for the negotiating process and its parties.

Try to Understand Where the Other Side Is Coming From

Sometimes the same deal can "smell" a lot better to the other side, simply by showing a little courtesy and sensitivity.

After months of agonizing back and forth while negotiating with the New Jersey Nets for all-star power forward Buck Williams, we were finally an inch away from making a deal that would pay Buck nearly $1.5 million per year. I was impatient to close this thing, as was Buck Williams. As we went into our umpteenth meeting, I figured the day had come when I could finally push them into signing the agreement.

I was pressuring them pretty hard when the Nets head owner said to me, "Donald, I don't want to seem personal, but do you make this kind of money in a year?" I looked at him like he was crazy. "Of course not," I said. "Not even close." The owner said, "Thanks. I was just curious."

After the meeting ended, I asked David Falk, who had been in the meeting with me, "What did he mean by that?" "What he meant," David chuckled, "is that one point five million dollars is a lot of money. They need another day to feel comfortable about paying somebody that much. They need another day to feel good about the deal." He was right, of course, and if I had been a little more sensitive about the situation, I could have figured that out for myself, for I had forgotten what the best negotiations are all about: striking a deal that everyone feels good about. Knowing from the start that there is such a point—where all interests converge and are served—is the secret of the best deal makers in business.

CHAPTER SIX

HOW TO DEAL WITH DIFFICULT CLIENTS

I once heard a fable about a scorpion and a water buffalo, which illustrates something significant about the client relationship. The scorpion, who wished to cross a river, said to the water buffalo, "This river is too wide and too deep for me to cross over it. Can I ride across on your back?"

"Of course not," the water buffalo replied. "If I let you get on my back, you will sting me and I will die."

"But that would be a stupid thing for me to do," the scorpion said. "If I sting you and you drown, I will drown as well."

The scorpion's logic prevailed, and the water buffalo allowed him to mount his back. Halfway across the river, the scorpion did indeed sting him. As the water buffalo started losing consciousness, he said to the scorpion, "Here we both are about to drown in this river. I don't understand. Why did you sting me?"

"Because," the scorpion replied, "it is my nature to sting."

Just as the scorpion's innate temperament predetermined his be-havior, the same can be said about clients. In fact, once people become clients, they begin to behave in certain predictable ways.

For instance, clients tend to be suspicious about the quality of the services they are receiving, no matter how good these services hap-pen to be. Their suspicions are usually sublimated so that the rela-tionship is not affected, but deep down inside there is a feeling that maybe the grass is a little bit greener at your competitor's.

Fees are another sore spot. Even when clients know they are getting their money's worth or better, they can't help feeling that maybe they are being a little bit overcharged. (Examine your own attitudes toward your lawyer or accountant and you will see what I mean.)

Deep-seated feelings of this sort add up to what I've come to think of as client nature—or the sometimes frighteningly predictable ways in which people, once they become clients, tend to behave, whether it's your oldest, most trusted client, or someone who just walked in the front door.

Understanding the Nature of the Beast

Later in this chapter, truly difficult client personalities will come into play, but first I'd like to examine the ways in which all clients can sometimes seem to be difficult.

What you must remember is that you are primarily dealing with difficult *problems,* not difficult people. This may not take the sting out of a cruel remark or make a perpetual whiner any more pleasant to be around, but it may help you begin to come to grips with what seems to be impossible behavior. The key to dealing with difficult client problems is to recognize client nature when you see it.

Once you begin to get a handle on client nature, you will not only be able to anticipate your clients' responses to just about any situation, you will also be able to avoid misunderstandings, hidden resentments, and communication breakdowns. The following is a list of the most common ways in which client nature tends to manifest itself:

1.   Clients, by nature, aren't appreciative.

Some clients are extremely appreciative, but most are not people who will send you a thank you note. This is because most clients are not aware of the "behind the scenes" expertise from which they benefit. That's why they hired you. For example, if a lawyer draws up a will for his or her client, no matter how complex the estate, the appreciation usually does not extend beyond payment of a bill for services rendered. If that same lawyer and client engage in a court battle together, the likelihood of receiving at least a pat on the back is far greater. The client not only has a clearer sense of the lengths to which his or her representative has gone to get the job done, but also feels more a part of the team effort.

Still, no client owes you his or her appreciation. Remembering this will help you to ward off your own resentments and to get on with the business at hand.

2.   Clients, by nature, expect your appreciation.

Clients may not be appreciative of your efforts, but they do expect you to behave as if *you* appreciate having them as clients. This manifests itself in a variety of ways, but more often than not it comes down to proving yourself to the client. Big and small clients alike want to feel as though they are extremely important to you, that you would drop everything to deal with their concerns first. When clients sense that you don't feel they are important enough, they will either start testing you with unnecessary requests or, even worse, begin to build an unspoken resentment toward you.

You can circumvent this demand for attention by anticipating it. The unexpected, out-of-the-ordinary gesture always speaks the loudest. A CPA I know once had to call his biggest client at home. Rather than being annoyed, the client was delighted—and impressed—that this CPA was plowing through his problems on a Sunday afternoon. From that point on, the CPA intentionally arranged weekend phone calls and after-hours home delivery of documents to this particular client.

3. Some clients, by nature, have tunnel vision.

Our clients number among the most gifted athletes in the world. They didn't get to where they are by being generalists. The flip side of excelling in a narrow pursuit is tunnel vision, which can severely distort judgment.

In our business, this often manifests in clients' conviction that because they can hit a tennis ball or dunk a basketball that they are qualified as experts on licensing, endorsements, PR, and promotions.

Once you understand what your clients don't understand, you will be better equipped to deal with their particular form of tunnel vision and head it off accordingly.

4. Some clients, by nature, tend to take advantage.

The client relationship is like any other: It needs boundaries and a clear set of expectations in order to work. In an undefined client relationship, the tendency is for the client to take advantage of your goodwill. He or she does not do it deliberately; the exploitation just develops.

One of the best creative directors in New York advertising once told me about his first big copywriting job. The client was wild about his work and the account was very secure. One day the client made an amazing request: He wanted the writer to pen a love letter to his current girlfriend. A year and about thirty love letters later, the copywriter finally put an end to it.

As I mentioned in the previous chapter, the key to avoiding being an indentured servant is to set mutual goals and parameters up front that both you and the client can live with.

5. Sometimes even the best clients, by nature, can be small and petty.

We were once in a board meeting when the secretary for Jerry Solomon, who was our head of men's tennis at the time, came in and told him that one of his biggest clients was on the phone.

"He has to talk to you right away," she said. "It's extremely urgent."

He came back in shaking his head and relayed the following exchange: The client had said, "I'm at the Toronto airport. My plane leaves in twenty minutes but the ticket agent here won't give me the seat that I want in first class. I want seat 2B, and she says it's taken, that I have to sit in 2A. I want you to talk to her. If you don't get me 2B, I'm not getting on that plane, and I'm going to skip the press conference and the tournament."

Since we had already assured his appearance, this was tantamount to blackmail. If it had been me, I might have been tempted to call his bluff. Fortunately, it wasn't, and his manager's cooler head prevailed.

"Listen," he said to the client, "go up to this woman and politely explain to her who you are. Tell her you need an aisle seat for leg room and ask her if she would please trade with the other person. If this doesn't work, have her call me and I'll talk to her."

Of course, the woman immediately gave him the seat, and we never heard back from him.

6. Clients, by nature, are often naive, impractical, or unrealistic.

We represented the young basketball player Kermit Washington the year he was drafted in the first round by the Los Angeles

Lakers. I flew out to Los Angeles with Kermit to negotiate with the Lakers owner, Jack Kent Cooke. During the flight, as I was explaining to Kermit what we would be looking for, he said to me, "I only want a contract for the years that I actually play." I wasn't sure that I had heard him correctly. "What do you mean?" I said. He said, "I don't want anything guaranteed or promised unless I'm going to do it. If I get hurt and can't play, I don't want to be paid."

This was *not* the typical player response to a six-year guaranteed no-cut contract. Apparently there was no room in Kermit's value system for him to be paid for something he didn't do or earn.

I asked Kermit to let me finalize the negotiations anyway. On the way back I said, "Kermit, I appreciate your idealism and your strong values, but I want to protect you from yourself here. You're going to get married in a month. What about your wife? What if you have children?" It took me two or three meetings, but I finally convinced him to change his mind and accept the guaranteed contract.

A funny thing happened. Kermit played in the league for thirteen years and played injury-free for the first ten years.

During the final year of his last three-year contract, he was injured and had to sit out the entire season. According to the terms of the guaranteed contract, the team still had to pay him. Kermit refused the money. I said, "Kermit, for God's sake, you have two kids. Accept the payments and stop all of this." He finally acquiesced, but in his own inimitable style; he called up the owner, Larry Weinberg, and stated, "I'm going to make it up to you. If you still want me next year, I'll play for nothing."

A year later Kermit came back strong from his injury and though he wanted to play for free, he was required by NBA commissioner David Stern to accept the league's minimum wage of $50,000. True story, but there are not many Kermit Washingtons in professional sports!

There are many other ways, of course, in which some clients can be difficult all the time, and all clients can be difficult some of the time. The point is to recognize client nature for what it is and then be able to deal with it in that light. The sting may hurt terribly, but as much as you might love to, you really can't blame the scorpion for doing what comes naturally.

The Big Four

Like paying bills, dealing with difficult clients is a fact of business life, not a pleasant one perhaps, but not a reason to change careers. There are some clients who do have the ability to make us question the businesses we are in. These are the truly difficult clients. These are the people who sometimes make us hate our business when what we really hate is dealing with them.

If you step back and recall the difficult clients you have had over your career you will see some patterns emerge. Although I'm generally not one to divide the world into categories, I have found that there are at least four basic client types that plague every kind of client business: the *bully,* the *know-it-all,* the *whiner,* and the *pleaser.*

The bully and the know-it-all, of course, intimidate with aggressive behavior. Frankly, with these clients, you've got a bull's-eye on your back. These people are particularly prone to taking out their hostilities on people who depend on them. As someone who is paid for services rendered, you make a dandy target.

At the other end of the spectrum, the pleaser and the whiner taunt you with a far more complex and subtle form of behavior. All have an equal capacity for making your life an absolute hell, unless you are prepared to deal with their "eccentricities."

The Bully

The bully is the same guy who kicked sand in your face at the beach, only now he or she sits on the other side of the desk from you and hurls threats and insults. Everyone has dealt with bullies or tyrants in their business lives, and when the bully comes in the form of a client, he or she can make your life miserable. Bully clients tend to be orators by nature and their orations usually end with some version of ". . . or I'll find someone who can." They also tend to fall into one of two subcategories: *weak kings* and *little Napoleons.*

Weak kings present an interesting special case because they may not be bullies at heart, but outside events have turned them into dangerous adversaries. If, for instance, your client is a corporation and your contact there is having problems unrelated to your relationship, be prepared to be the scapegoat anyway. When this is the case, try to be clear to your client about what you see happening. Don't start out by saying, "You're on a losing streak and you're blaming everyone else around you" because your words won't fall on very receptive ears. Instead, tell him how you are upset because of certain things he has said and done, focusing on your condition rather than on his miserable behavior.

The result will probably be an either/or response. Either you will penetrate, in which case the relationship will resume some semblance of normalcy, or you won't, in which case you will simply hasten the inevitable.

As far as the little Napoleons are concerned, clients don't have to be big to be bullies or small to be Napoleonic but merely convinced that life has shortchanged them. Napoleons use louder and meaner methods to get their way. Their way of gaining control, paradoxically, is by losing control. They explode, everyone takes cover, and they are in charge again.

What do you do with these walking time bombs? Admittedly I am not an expert here, as I tend to fight fire with fire, with the result often being a conflagration.

Several years ago we signed Masters champion Ray Floyd, who was to be the flagship of our fledgling golf division. Ray had been with our biggest competitor, International Management Group (IMG) for seventeen years. A key ingredient in the move was Ray's wife, Maria, who seemed to call most of the business shots. Maria had ambitions for Ray, and we offered him the chance to be number one in our golf division. Five or six years later, when he would no longer be competing, our plan was to bring him into our organization to head up our golf program. After a year and a half in which I thought we had done a pretty good job for Ray, Maria and Ray came into my office for a 9 A.M. meeting to discuss extending our representation agreement. Typically, I was running behind, and I didn't usher them into my office until fifteen minutes after nine.

Ray is the gentlest guy in the world, but Maria had been stoking his fires for the entire fifteen minutes. By the time he entered my office, smoke was coming out of his ears. His opening comment was, "Donald, when I was with IMG, I was never kept waiting by Mark McCormack. This is a hell of a way to treat a client."

It was early in the morning and I was fresh as a tiger. I said to myself, "This is too much." I got so angry it surprised me. I said, "Hey, look Ray, are we here to talk business, or are you here to give speeches and lectures? I'm sorry I was late. I was on an overseas phone call. My fault—I apologize. Do you want to talk about the time of the meeting or your business? It's your choice."

He was right, and I didn't handle it very well.

One minute into the meeting Ray clammed up and Maria took over. She accused me of not keeping our promises to Ray. She accused one of our associates of lying to her. Now all of a sudden I was the referee.

Miraculously, the meeting ended on a positive note because we had done a very good marketing job for Ray Floyd. We had made him about $350,000 in a year when he hadn't won a single tournament. At the end of the discussion Ray and I shook hands and agreed that we would extend our working relationship for another year.

A month later, one week before his option to extend was to expire, we received a three-paragraph letter from Ray (but which I suspect was written by Maria) saying he was terminating our agreement.

How well did I handle the situation? If the final outcome is any indication, I would have to say horribly. Dealing with bullies takes an enormous amount of self-control because the tendency is to kick sand right back at them. The problem is you can't and have any real success over the long term. You've got to get them back to your agenda, no matter how hard they try to sidetrack you. Here are some guidelines for dealing with bullies which admittedly I sometimes preach better than I practice:

• *Don't show fear.* Especially with Napoleons, fear suggests weakness and incompetence. Never look or act intimidated by a bully (even if you are).

• *Always have your act together.* A bully is unhappy to have to rely on you in the first place. Don't make it worse by being unprepared and disorganized.

• *Never ramble.* A bully generally detests chitchat and lengthy presentations. He is impatient by nature. Get to your point quickly.

The Know-It-Alls

For the know-it-alls, control is the secret to life. They long to believe that if people would listen to them more attentively (and quit screwing up as a result) the world could be that well-ordered place it was meant to be.

The toughest part about having know-it-alls as clients is that, if left to their own devices, they will rob you of the opportunity to do your job. Although you were hired because of your expertise, know-it-alls, on a certain level, behave as if you were overrated, superfluous, or just plain dumb.

As I mentioned in an earlier chapter, the toughest client we ever had in this regard was Ivan Lendl. As Lendl headed toward the top rung of the tennis world, he was also becoming an "expert" in real estate, promotions, and finances. His attitude was essentially "if ProServ can do it, then surely I can do it better."

One night, over dinner, he and I got into an intense argument about how to promote and sell a tennis tournament in Washington. He had opinions on everything: ticket prices, volunteers, ball boys, hotels, and transportation. His criticisms of our approach to tournaments were thinly disguised.

I said, "Look, Ivan, we've been running tournaments for seventeen years, an average of twenty a year. I don't pretend to be the only expert on the subject, but I do think I know a lot more about it than you do. However, if you are so keen on running a tennis event, I'll find you one to run yourself."

And we did. We arranged for him to play in an exhibition match in Hartford. I told him he could promote the entire event, waive his appearance fee, and take all the profits—or the loss. He readily agreed. One month before the event was to take place, it was canceled because of lack of promotions and a lack of ticket sales in the Hartford area.

Like bullies, know-it-alls also come in two standard types, *Mr. Right* and *Mr. Wrong.* The problem with dealing with the Mr. Rights of the world is that they often do indeed know it all, or at least most of it. They have such an instinct for their own needs, the frustration often comes in having to admit they may have a point.

I've heard, for instance, that Ernest Gallo of the Gallo wineries, is the most difficult client in advertising. Why? Because he routinely sends his agencies back to the drawing board five, ten, fifteen times before agreeing to a campaign concept, if he agrees to it at all. Agency executives who have worked for Gallo—and there have been twenty in the past forty years—all admit that he knows what he is doing—and is unfailingly kind in his critiques. So far, though, no one has gotten a sense of how to deal with him in the long term.

How does one best deal with a Mr. Right? For starters:

• *Listen.* Mr. Right will trust you more if he or she feels you are attentive, and you may actually learn something.

• *Play it back, and make sure that he or she knows that you "got it."* Mr. Rights are sticklers for effective communication. They tell rather than ask: Give them a sign that you're on their wavelength.

• *Most important, accept the fact that you will have to defer to Mr. Right more often than not.* If this sounds impossible to do, keep in mind that two Mr. Rights make a wrong. Find someone in your organization who is temperamentally equipped to handle this kind of client. It takes a healthy ego to withstand repeated assaults from any know-it-all, and all the more so when they happen to be right. If you are combative yourself, you are probably not long for this kind of client.

In an odd way, *Mr. Wrong* is much easier to work with. He pretends to know it all and clearly doesn't. We've all had discussions at dinner parties with people who don't know what they are talking about (and insist on talking anyway) but these are the amateurs. The Mr. Wrongs of the world are professional phonies. They speak with great conviction, tend to be extremely glib, and are consumed with the desire to be *viewed* as authorities.

A few years ago, a friend of mine who owns a sports magazine promoted its advertising director to publisher. The new publisher was aware of "being in over his head" and he developed some strange habits. At meetings he would either dominate with rambling tangents that burned up all of the meeting time or he would become mute, except to repeat the last sentence that everyone said. The situation worsened until he became a laughing stock. Within a year, the publisher was fired.

I have found the Peter Principle turns many clients into Mr. Wrongs. They are pampered and promoted, find themselves in over their heads, and compensate by becoming know-it-alls. What can you do with a Mr. Wrong?

● *Resist nailing him or her to the wall.* With Mr. Wrongs you can have a long and wonderful client relationship by allowing them to pretend they are right in all the unimportant matters, even when you both know they are wrong.

● *Meet one on one, whenever possible.* Mr. Wrong wastes your time in direct proportion to the number of people in the room. For some reason, the more witnesses there are, the more he or she tends to pontificate. Meet in private where the client doesn't feel the need to show off.

● *Like it or not, your goal must be to protect Mr. Wrong from him- or herself.* The relationship works best when it's conspiratorial. Both of you know when the client is wrong, but if you keep it to yourself, he or she, in turn, will always go along with you on key issues.

All know-it-alls, be they infuriatingly right or infuriatingly wrong, aren't intentionally trying to make life difficult for you, but are merely trying to deal with their own needs, which, for Mr. Right, is control, and for Mr. Wrong, is the *appearance* of control. Keep this in mind, and you will be able to enhance your personal effectiveness with these clients.

The Whiner

Whiners are the human version of chalk squealing on a blackboard. No matter what you do, it's never enough. They are the Rodney Dangerfields of the business world. In their own mind, they never get enough respect.

For the most part, whiners feel disempowered. By casting aspersions on everyone around, whiners/complainers not only gain a sense of power but also camouflage the inadequacies that haunt them. In dealing with whiners, I think there are several considerations. First, is this out-of-the-ordinary behavior? In our business, for instance, when the complaint quotient dramatically increases with one of our clients, I tend to look for other factors that may be adversely affecting another part of his or her life: a nagging injury or an unexplained losing streak. In these cases, I try to hold a mirror up to the client— help the client see him or herself as others do and compel the client to examine the real source of whatever it is that is making him or her unhappy. This works with an amazing degree of effectiveness. The "unnatural" whiner/complainer is usually receptive to this approach.

The "natural" whiners are a tougher nut to crack. What I try to do in these cases is overwhelm them with independent confirmation of reality. For six years we represented Harold Solomon, who was a very solid-ranked player and a real fighter on the tennis court. For some reason Solly always felt he never got his due and he complained incessantly as a result. When his playing days were coming to an end, he told the people representing him he wanted to be a television commentator, which is a dream of a lot of ex-athletes, but one that rarely comes true. In Solly's case, he wasn't as articulate or as analytical as he thought he was. He was told his talents lay elsewhere. For weeks we heard from people close to him that they heard nothing but that his abilities were being shortchanged, how the networks were playing other favorites, and how no one had any interest in his career after tennis.

Ultimately, Solomon left ProServ and joined IMG. Evidently the whining about a career in television continued. I was told that IMG finally arranged a series of network auditions for him and asked the networks to provide written critiques of Solly's tryouts. Needless to say, it did not go well and with this independent confirmation of the fact in writing, the IMG executives were at last able to stem the whining on this particular subject.

One of the big dangers in dealing with whiners is that oftentimes they may have a genuine beef. As with bullies, the great challenge in dealing with whiners and complainers is separating substance, which may be legitimate, from the grating, irritating form in which it is delivered. To make solving this problem as easy on yourself as it can be, try the following.

● *Make it a game.* Use your willpower, not to outcomplain, but to focus on substance, if there is any. If there isn't, don't let it go unchallenged. Let the client know when his or her continuing complaints are unfounded.

● *Take copious notes at meetings which you can use later on.* Hard evidence is often required to tame a wild complaint. Also, complaints ("he doesn't call me enough") seem a little pettier when they are seen in writing.

● *Collaborate.* Show the client that mistakes can happen, that problems can be solved, and that he or she need not feel impotent because the world is imperfect. Bring the client to the center of the problem-solving process and this will break his or her automatic chalk-on-the-blackboard response.

The Aim-to-Pleasers

The aim-to-pleasers are great in the short term, but over the long haul they need careful handling. They can bankrupt a company or throw an entire project into disarray just because they don't want to hurt someone's feelings, make a decision, or give a straight answer when that's what's needed.

Pleasers would rather die than confront someone with an uncomfortable truth, and client relationships, in many respects, depend on a continuous exchange of truths, both comfortable and uncomfortable.

For a number of years we represented former Wimbledon finalist Roscoe Tanner. Roscoe would tell you anything you wanted to hear, in part because he didn't like confrontations and in part because he didn't like to be chastised. Roscoe's coach, Dennis Ralston, a former top-ranked player who now coaches Chris Evert, was also one of our clients. One time Dennis called me from a tennis club in Santa Barbara, California, and said, "I want to play doubles with Tanner in the upcoming Washington tournament, but Roscoe won't give me a straight answer. Will you find out from him, once and for all, whether or not he wants to be my doubles partner?"

Before I even hung up, Roscoe was calling on another line. He was at the same club, calling from a different room, and he said, "Donald, I really don't want to play doubles next week in Washington at all."

I felt like a den mother. "Roscoe," I said, "just tell Dennis what you just told me, but tell him now so he can get another partner."

"Okay," Tanner said.

Needless to say, I later got the privilege myself of telling Ralston what his own pupil couldn't bring himself to say, but, by that time, the Washington draw had already been made, and Ralston was stuck without a partner.

Another time Roscoe, Stan Smith, and their wives were coming to Washington for a tournament. I had invited them to stay at our house. "We'd love to," Roscoe kept telling me, but his wife Nancy kept telling Stan's wife, Margie, that she didn't want to stay with us.

Every time I talked to Roscoe, though, he'd make a remark like, "See you next Monday in Washington." Well, this nonsense went on until about eleven o'clock on the Sunday evening before the tournament. It must have killed Roscoe to make the call that evening, but he finally did—from a downtown Washington hotel. The hotel, he said, was more convenient because it was closer to the tournament. The poor guy just could not bring himself to tell me anything he thought I didn't want to hear.

The important thing to remember about aim-to-pleasers is that they can't say no. And because they can't say no—or deliver bad news or disagree—they end up getting into situations where they are either in over their heads, going through the motions (until they back out), or are committed to something they don't really want to do and blame you for it as a result. To compound the problem, it is easy to impose on clients like these because they offer the path of least resistance.

There is a terrible "false economy" about taking advantage of a pleaser. Say you are a lawyer and want your "pleaser" client to gather up some background material for a case you are presenting on his behalf, and you need the material by Monday.

The aim-to-pleaser agrees to do about ninety-six hours worth of work in forty-eight hours and over the weekend to boot. When he fails to get it done, and the ripple effect ravages all of your other scheduling, you realize you would have been far better off anticipating his unrealistic desires to accommodate you and devising a realistic workload as a result.

Although the aim-to-pleasers' well-meaningness can seem harmless enough, it can be terribly detrimental to any service business. After all, your job is to keep the client happy. It's like flying without instruments.

Pleasers can also be difficult because their reluctance to hurt others and their fear of getting hurt themselves renders them incapable of making the tough decision. Getting a pleaser to take a bold stance is virtually impossible. And when that pleaser is your client—and decisions have to be made—you can be put in a real bind.

I cannot tell you how many times we've had clients agree to tournament schedules, exhibitions, or endorsement appearances only to hear at the last minute from their mothers, fathers, wives, or girlfriends that they won't be showing up. Sometimes you never hear from them directly. And guess who gets the blame when the appearance or event is all messed up?

Suppose, for instance, an architect can't get a straight answer from the young couple for whom he is building a house. The couple feels ambivalent about some of the design features, but they can't stand the idea of criticizing the architect's work—of saying they don't like some of his solutions. As a result, the unhappiness comes out in other ways down the road, like a quarrel over the size of the architect's fee, for instance, or design modifications that have to be made after construction is already underway. Either way, the architect ends up being the enemy.

In dealing with the aim-to-pleasers's personality as best you can:

● *Give the pleasers a choice.* If they can't say no, it's important to give them other ways to say the *N* word. Rather than say, "Do you want to do this?" say, "Would you rather do this or would you rather do that?"

● *Filter the pleaser's remarks through your own awareness of his or her well-meaningness.* A slight hesitation in the voice of an aim-to-pleaser is a resounding "no" in the voice of someone else. Also, what does he or she joke about? Aim-to-pleasers often use humor to soften their true feelings.

• *Aim-to-pleasers need positive reinforcement to feel comfortable in explaining themselves.* Tell them often that you value their opinion.

• *Never let them commit to anything unrealistic:* a deadline, a project, an appearance, even your fee!

The easier you make it for the aim-to-pleaser to express his or her true feelings, the easier you are going to make it for yourself ultimately.

There are, of course, many other difficult client types—the second-guesser, the blame-thrower, and so on. But the main thing to remember in dealing with any difficult client is that the same things that work throughout the business world—patience, persistence, being a good listener, and having the ability to separate form from substance—work here as well. It is only the extreme degree to which these qualities come into play that sets apart the care and feeding of these particular people from other business relationships.

In this respect, perhaps the most useful overall advice that I can offer in dealing with all difficult clients is to recognize up front that the relationship most probably will have a preordained shelf life. Over the years we have had many clients who would have tried the patience of Job, but I have come to realize during this period that not only am I not Job, I don't want to be Job.

Ironically, recognizing up front that sooner or later, through no fault of your own, the relationships with chronically difficult clients usually come to an end, will help you to manage the relationships better.

CHAPTER SEVEN

DEALING WITH CORPORATE CLIENTS

Most of us tend to think of clients as individuals. Yet by far the major consumer of services in this country, from telecommunications to tennis tournaments, are not individuals at all but groups of individuals—corporations.

The relationship between corporations and their hundreds of independent suppliers of goods and services is the classic illustration of symbiosis. The corporation needs the smaller companies which can provide specialized services and expertise with far greater skill and efficiency than if the corporation were to attempt to do everything itself. Like pilot fish swimming along with a shark, these "specialists" owe their very existence to the larger corporations.

Corporations as clients present a fascinating case in dealing with clients in general. On the one hand, since companies are no more than groups of individuals, the same things that work in dealing with individual clients should also apply, and often do. On the other hand, when one introduces group dynamics, herd mentality, and other realities of corporate life into the equation, this can change everything—and often does.

Over the years we have had numerous corporate clients, mostly in our capacity of television programmers and packagers of sporting events. I have found the complexity of dealing with corporations often frustrating but endlessly fascinating. The key to success in having corporations as clients—to the extent there is a key—lies in understanding the ways and situations in which companies are most likely to behave like companies—and the influence this exerts over the individuals who work for them.

The Nature of the Beast—Corporately

Just as there is a "client nature"—predictable ways in which individual clients will behave—the same is true of corporations. Whether you are soliciting a company's business for the first time or have had a corporation as a client for years, it helps to keep in mind that all companies, even the best run, are bureaucracies to some degree, and suffer from bureaucratic tendencies. If at the beginning you can understand and appreciate some of the roadblocks this bureaucracy will almost certainly create, you will be better prepared mentally and emotionally to deal with them.

The Morass Roadblock

It is very rare for any corporate decision to be made unilaterally by one person, even if that person has the authority to do so. There are systems and procedures to contend with, and few corporate executives would want to stick out their singular necks anyway. The way the game is played is this: Spread the responsibility; then, if anything goes wrong, you can also spread the blame. This creates entanglements for anyone trying to do business from the outside. You soon learn that getting even the simplest thing done can often take great time and effort.

When we first began to develop a relationship with the Coca-Cola Company, one of their executives told us right up front, "We're a fragmented company, and you'll have to commit to jumping through a lot of hoops if you want to do business with us." We thought he was exaggerating the truth, but as we found out, he was actually sugarcoating it.

We made a conscious decision to go after Coke's business anyway. We spent a year running all over the world talking to every Coke executive imaginable and not getting anywhere. I was fed up, but the calmer heads of some of my associates prevailed. Then one day a few weeks later I got a call from Coke's head of marketing, who said, "Okay, you've paid your dues. Come on in and talk to us." At the meeting he invited the brand managers from every division of Coke—Classic Coke, New Coke, Diet Coke, Fresca, Tab, you name it. We finally had our day in court.

The year of running around the world apparently had been our price of admission. It showed Coke that we were serious about wanting to do business with them, and, in fact, we have since made some significant deals.

At least Coke was savvy enough and helpful enough to appreciate the difficulties inherent in dealing with them (or any other large corporation, for that matter). They told us up front what to expect, and we were able to make a choice as to whether we wanted to proceed. More often, this is something you end up having to discover for yourself. The result can be that you prematurely abandon your effort, not because you are no longer willing to pay the price of admission, but because you simply don't know what that price is going to be.

The "Playing It Safe" Roadblock

Companies by nature tend toward conservatism. They often owe their very existence to some famous product that has been around for years, and they know they can increase business by 15 percent every year merely by raising their prices. It doesn't pay them, either collectively or individually, to take risks.

The result of this corporate conservatism is something of a paradox: The more innovative or inventive you are, the less chance your ideas have of getting off the ground or even getting a fair hearing.

I once saw a film on advertising entitled *Risk vs. Reward,* which illustrated this paradox beautifully. It was about how all great advertising depends on someone being willing to take a risk. The film's hypothesis was that suppose Hathaway, the famous shirtmaker, had reacted like a typical corporation when presented with the idea for its classic "Man in the Hathaway shirt" print campaign.

The film opens with an artist working up an advertising sketch. The sketch shows a successful man posing in a white shirt. But what attracts your attention is that the man is wearing a black patch over one eye.

The artist first shows the sketch to the company researcher who says, "This looks good to me, and 62 percent of the solid shirts we sell are white. My only reservation is that our shirts also come in other solid colors." So the artist goes back and adds the tag line: "Also available in blue, pink, and yellow."

He then takes his revised sketch to the advertising manager. "I like it," the manager says, "but do you think someone might infer that we only sell solid-colored shirts? We also have a full line of striped and plaid shirts, you know." Once again the artist goes back to the drawing board and sketches in little boxes showing shirt cloth in pin-striped and plaid patterns.

Next he's sent up to the marketing director, who looks at the sketch and says, "You certainly have all the bases covered. But there is something crucially wrong with this ad. Men don't buy shirts. Their wives buy them for them."

The artist goes back a final time and sketches a woman in the background, lovingly looking over the shoulder of her man.

Now all that is needed is for the company president to sign off on the ad. He stares at it a long time before replying. But finally he shakes his head. "I like it," he says unconvincingly. "I just feel it's off the mark. How many one-eyed men buy our shirts anyway?"

This film obviously is meant to be entertaining, but makes the serious point that the danger for any corporation is that you can "safe" an idea to death. If companies didn't take a chance once in a while, Jocko would never promote Eveready batteries and Isuzu's now-famous liar's campaign would never have gotten off the drawing board. Nevertheless, it's best when dealing with a corporation to assume—and to base your selling strategy—on the fact that the more unconventional you are or the more you depart from a company's own image of itself, the less chance you have of making any real headway.

The "Team Player" Roadblock

A large corporation is like a great battleship. It is very hard to overcome inertia and get the company moving in the right direction, but once you do, it is just as hard to stop its momentum or even alter its course. In other words, the hard part is *getting on board*. Once you are there, it is almost equally hard to get swept over the side. Just make sure you don't rock the boat.

This is a roadblock only because for one to resist rocking the boat is sometimes a lot more difficult than it might sound. People who run independent businesses are by definition more "independent minded." They are constitutionally less able to fit into the team concept than those who have chosen to go the corporate route. Once you are invited to be part of the team, it is as a team player that you are expected to behave. This demands a whole new mind-set and way of looking at things.

For small independent businesses, the ends often must justify the means out of necessity. In large corporations, they almost never do: How you got there is just as important as where you end up.

Brian Cowgill, the former managing director for Britain's ITV television, became the victim of these two antithetical approaches. Brian had the mind for corporate life but more the soul of an entrepreneur. Once, he secretly negotiated to wrest the rights to *Dallas,* the hottest rated TV show at the time in England, away from the rival BBC, which had owned the rights since the nighttime soap had begun.

The problem was that Cowgill's negotiations were so secret he neglected to tell even his boss. When the BBC got wind that ITV was bidding up the price for *Dallas,* the head of the BBC called Cowgill's boss and said, "Everyone tells us that ITV is secretly negotiating for *Dallas.* What's the story?" Cowgill's boss honestly said, "I don't know what you're talking about. This is obviously a totally unfounded rumor."

Ultimately, ITV won the rights to *Dallas,* probably the deal of the decade for the network. When Cowgill went public with his coup, he got fired for his efforts. Although no one quarreled with his results, his means had publicly embarrassed his boss and had violated the "old school tie" network in England.

To represent corporations, part of you needs to think like a corporation. You always want to be alert, for instance, to the possibility that a corporate client might be put in an awkward position, and you must take whatever steps necessary to prevent that from happening. Once again anticipation and the consequences of your actions are important factors.

Last year, during the semifinals of the DuPont all-American tennis championships, Jimmy Connors began suffering from heat prostration. After the match he could barely eat, and it was clear to us that there was a possibility he wouldn't be physically able to play in the finals the next day.

That night we went to the DuPont officials, told them that Jimmy was sick and that he might not be able to play, or if he did play the match, he might have to withdraw before it was over.

Jimmy tried to play, but early in the match he had to drop out and default. He was so sick he couldn't even make it to the awards ceremony.

Since we had anticipated what might happen, DuPont wasn't as disturbed as they might have been. In fact, we had already prepared a statement from Jimmy that was read at the awards ceremony. We put the best face on this otherwise unfortunate development. It was a simple gesture, but it showed DuPont we were doing our utmost to protect their interests, and to keep an otherwise very positive program from turning into a negative one.

Don't Ever Think You've Figured It Out

Companies have their own secret agendas, and because of the people and the politics involved, the subtexts can become so complicated that often an outsider could not possibly figure out the company's motivations for its actions.

One time the president of the Grow Chemical Company contacted us and asked us to put together a tennis event for him. He put up $250,000 for prize money and television ads and some additional sums to secure the facilities—not a lot of money perhaps, but a considerable sum considering that none of Grow's products were for sale to the public.

We found out later that the main reason for this tournament was that the president of the company had planned a seminar for all his top executives, and he was determined to attract his business idol, former Secretary of the Treasury William Simon, as the featured speaker. He learned that Simon really enjoyed tennis and so he had us create the "Grow Doubles Championship" at Woodlands, Texas, primarily to make attending his seminar more attractive to Bill Simon!

Reaching the Right Person

For anyone who must deal with corporations, the biggest problem, by far, is reaching the right person—someone who appreciates your needs and understands your questions and who is willing and able to get you answers even if those answers aren't always the ones you want to hear.

You have to pay attention to figure out who the real movers and shakers are within the company—who has the boss's ear or who is relied on to get certain things done.

Getting to the right person is usually a function of starting at the top and gingerly working your way down, all the time using your common sense.

For instance, we used to deal with David Foster when he was chairman of Colgate-Palmolive. One of the percs he had in this powerful position was to be in charge of anything dealing with sports. He was the head of the whole company, but he was the one who made the decisions relating to sports promotions.

At the other end of the spectrum is a company like Coca-Cola, which maintains such a fine balance between its brands, its various operations, and its independent bottlers, there really is no such thing as the right person. The company is internally so decentralized it is more a process than a person that gives you the approval.

The right "guy" for us at HBO, it turned out, has really been "two guys," Michael Fuchs, the president, and Seth Abraham, vice president of their sports programming. We know that when we can get both Michael and Seth to commit, it will happen—guaranteed.

The point, I guess, is not to assume that the highest level person is necessarily the right contact for you. On the other hand, you don't want to be passed down the ladder from rung to rung until you're dealing with someone in the mail room. You have to know when you reach your ideal point of penetration. Usually this is a person who has been given the authority to make the decisions in your area and is also someone with whom, for whatever reason, you feel you can develop a personal chemistry and relationship.

In order to locate the right person for you within the corporation with the greatest success and efficiency, first you need to have a clear picture in your own mind of precisely what your needs are and who within the corporation is most likely to fulfill them. The vice president of sales may be your uncle, but if your needs lie in the advertising department, the most your uncle is going to be able to do for you is point you in the right direction.

That, in fact, is the next step: If you don't already know who the right person is, whom do you know who can point you in the right direction? Anyone you know within the company or who has worked for that company before can be a major ally in this regard, not because they are the ones to whom you should be speaking but because they should be able to suggest the right person.

When to Go to the Top

The chairman of a company is even more powerful than the typical corporate flowchart would indicate. The traditional pyramidal structure of a corporation, with the bottom employees at the wide base and the CEO at the very top, is really an inaccurate depiction. In reality, the pyramid should top out with the vice chairman of the board. Then, a mile or so higher, should be a separate box for the chairman. The old joke, of course, is that if there are ten members of the board of directors, the chairman gets eleven votes.

For outsiders seeking to do business with a corporation, the chairman is all-powerful, not simply because he or she is the "boss," but because it is the chairman who decides which decision-making powers are delegated to others—and to whom—and which ones are kept for him or herself.

When the element of time was first introduced into tennis tournaments, prescribing a specific amount of time for changeovers and service, I went directly to Reijiro Hattori, Seiko's chairman, and sold him on the idea of putting Seiko time clocks on the courts of all the Grand Prix tennis tournaments throughout the world. That particular promotion was so successful for Seiko, Mr. Hattori later came to us and asked us to create a tournament for Seiko. It has now become the biggest annual tennis event in Japan.

Usually, the chairman of the company does not get involved with the nitty-gritty, day-to-day realities of the business such as dealing with outside suppliers of services. Nevertheless, I believe very strongly in going right to the top for another reason. If the chairman is not the right person, and he or she probably isn't, you will learn that very quickly, but if the chairman is intrigued with your concept or business, his or her office will put you in touch with the right person within the corporation with whom you should be dealing. For an outsider, there is no more effective "cold call" than to begin with "The chairman of your company suggested I call you about . . ."

When Not to Go to the Top

One of the dangers of going to the top is that in doing so you may alienate the hands-on people who may have the ultimate decision-

making authority over your business. You can offend a lot of people
if they feel you are trying to ride on the coattails of a powerful
relationship you have. They can then intentionally or unintentionally
sabotage what might have otherwise been a pleasant and profitable
relationship.

Over the years, we have gotten very close with Akio Morita, the
chairman and founder of Sony. Mr. Morita is an electronics genius
who, among other things, invented the Walkman. He also happens
to love tennis, though we have never been able to translate this into
any business. Mr. Morita has very little hands-on involvement in
Sony promotions and advertising. Whenever we suggest anything to
him directly, he always puts us in touch with the Sony people in New
York, whom I think may see us more as Mr. Morita's friends with
a shared personal interest than as people with legitimate business
opportunities. Oddly, if Mr. Morita had less passion for tennis, we
would probably fare better.

It is still a valued friendship, of course, but from a business standpoint we might have done better if we had initiated our talks with
one of his key lieutenants who really is involved in the day-to-day
decisions about Sony promotions.

Even when you do have a sound relationship with the chairman,
you have to be very careful how you use it. Part of our dealings with
the sheik of Dubai involved our televising the tournament throughout the world. When our television crew arrived on the scene, they
discovered the local crew, with whom they had to work, was com-
posed almost entirely of fanatical Palestinians, who told them, quite
literally, "America is evil. We'd rather kill you than be forced to
work with you."

We were faced with a choice. Should we go back to the sheik and
demand a different crew? Or should we grit our teeth and try to find
some way to make this work?

The situation surrounding this whole event was so sensitive, we
decided, and I think quite rightly, that going to the sheik might

alienate not only the crew but the sheik as well. If you are a Palestinian fanatic, you are hardly going to change your approach to Americans simply because the sheik has told you to be friendly.

What we did instead was appeal to their professional pride. They happened to have some of the finest state-of-the-art television equipment anywhere. Once we had engaged them in a discussion of communication technology, we were able to say, "Listen, you are professionals and so are we. Let's try to make this tournament, out here in the middle of the desert, the best televised event imaginable."

Several days later, when it was time to leave, many members of the Palestinian crew actually thanked our crew for their help and cooperation.

Another reason you should sometimes think twice before going to the top is that the answer you get may not be the one you want. A personality trait that has caused me some problems over the years is that I believe I can talk myself into or out of almost anything. I have been proven wrong often enough that I should know better, but some lessons are harder to learn than others.

Several years ago, Bob Briner, who heads up our television company, and I were about to board a plane in Korea on our way to Taiwan, when I discovered that I had forgotten to get my Taiwan visa. Briner suggested that there was no way I was going to get into Taiwan without that visa. I figured I could talk my way in since we were, after all, going there on behalf of the Taiwanese Tennis Federation and as guests of the Taiwanese government.

When our plane landed, an official at the gate asked to see my visa. When I told him I didn't have one and politely explained my dilemma, he very politely said, "I'm sorry, but if you don't have a visa, we can't allow you into our country."

"You don't understand," I said. "I'm here because I'm representing your country's tennis federation."

When he still wouldn't acquiesce, I got angry and demanded to see the head of immigration immediately. About a half an hour later a portly, pleasant-looking gentleman in a military uniform came over and was introduced to us as the director of immigration for all of Taiwan.

"I'm so glad someone is here who can finally make a decision about this thing," I said. "We're already late, and I need to get to our embassy right away. We're going over to see the head of your sports federation. My name is Donald Dell, and I'm here to help organize Taiwan's first international tennis tournament."

All the while I was talking, this official was smiling at me and nodding his head. "Finally," I thought, "I'm making some headway." When I stopped talking, this gentleman continued to smile, nodded his head very politely, and said in broken English, "No wisa, no wisit."

"No, you don't understand," I said, and went through my story again. Again he listened very patiently and then smiled at me and said, "No wisa, no wisit."

Finally, about the fourth time through, it dawned on me. This fellow didn't understand a word of English. It also dawned on me that even if he did, it wasn't going to do me a bit of good, that without that visa, there was no way I was going to get into the country.

The final scene Briner recalls is my standing at the top of the plane's stairway, reading from my appointment book and yelling at him down on the ground, "And don't forget to see Mr. So-and-so at two-thirty, and make sure you call . . ."

The last scene I recall is my waving out the window to a bemused Briner as we began taxiing out to the runway on the continuing flight to Hong Kong.

The Corporate Mentor

What you are ideally seeking to find or develop within the corporation is a mentor—someone with whom you may not be dealing directly but, because he or she likes you or the work you do, will

watch out for your interests, advise you how to best accomplish your
aims, and even grease the internal wheels for you every once in a
while.

For several years we have had this sort of relationship with John
Lampe, senior vice president of advertising at Paine Webber. John
likes tennis and feels it is a good promotional vehicle for reaching
Paine Webber's clientele. Perhaps because of "bias," he is reluctant
to be the final decision maker directly related to all tennis promotions. Instead, he will say to us, "If you really believe in this, then
these are the three executives here you will have to convince."

We know going in whom we have to sell, and we respond accordingly. We try to convince them that what we want to do is right for
the company, and we know that if we are successful, these are the
people within Paine Webber who will give us the approval. For us,
Lampe is the perfect corporate mentor. Although he will rarely
unilaterally make a decision that is helpful to us, he will always point
us in the right direction.

You should solicit a corporate mentor in much the same way you
solicit an individual client. You want to cultivate someone you perceive as a potential mentor, not just as somebody you do business
with, but as a friend and an ally. You should seek to put the relationship on a personal friendship level. Establishing such a valuable ally
has worked for us over and over again.

The Corporate Mole

When our competitor, International Management Group, was
granted the right to represent the television rights to the Seoul Olympics, they attributed much of their success to what they referred to
internally as their "Mole in Seoul"—someone with access to the
committee's thinking who helped keep them informed about decisions relating to rights representation.

The "mole" is a very powerful and tricky relationship. It's analogous in many ways to the relationship that Watergate journalists Woodward and Bernstein had with "Deep Throat." In a sense, the mole acts almost as an internal spy.

You have to have total trust and confidence in what he or she is saying, that the mole is seeing everything plainly and has both yours and his or her company's best interest at heart.

It's a rare relationship, but most valuable.

The best example I can give from my own experience was a relationship we, as a company, had with the late Horst Dassler, whose father, Adi, founded the German athletic shoe empire, Adidas.

First and foremost, we respected Horst enormously. In my opinion he was the smartest sports businessman that I had ever dealt with. Horst, along with his mother and sisters, ran Adidas after his father died, and he was considered one of the great powers in sporting goods manufacturing, sports marketing, and sports in general (particularly international events such as the Olympics).

I can remember one meeting with Horst in Germany. At the time he was designing the A-15, Adidas's legendary three-striped light warm-up suit that revolutionized the athletic-wear industry and to a large extent the way people dressed throughout the world. Advising him was the famous French fashion designer Daniel Hechter.

I said to Horst, "These are tennis clothes. Why do you need a fashion designer?"

"You don't understand," he replied. "Our market isn't tennis players. These clothes are for coming out of your apartment on a Saturday morning and going around the corner to pick up your newspaper and buy some milk."

He understood his product in terms of who bought it and what it was really for. The warm-up suit was to be worn when you wanted to dress casually but still wanted to look great. It was at the forefront of the whole movement toward athletic wear becoming leisure wear.

A few sets were sent to Bill Cosby, who practically lived in them. For several years, any candid photograph of Bill Cosby showed him wearing an Adidas warm-up suit. Horst was selling leisure wear for people who felt a little sloppy wearing jeans and T-shirts.

Horst also understood that he wasn't in the shoe and clothing business as much as he was in the image business, which is why he would pay players like Ivan Lendl, Ilie Nastase, and Stan Smith unbelievable sums of money.

Stan Smith, in fact, was Horst's original entry into the American tennis shoe market. Stan had won Wimbledon in 1972, and he was the Great American Hope like Jack Nicklaus in golf. We were negotiating for Stan with Converse when Horst called to say that he wanted to sign Smith, and I jokingly replied, "You can't afford Stan." Horst immediately replied that we could, in effect, name our price.

Signing Smith with Adidas was a contract that has worked out for everyone, because the Stan Smith Adidas tennis shoe has become the top-selling tennis shoe in history. To expand their market further, Adidas did the unconventional by manufacturing a "Lady Smith" shoe—a shoe designed for women endorsed by a male tennis player!

Horst constantly made decisions like that, decisions that sounded peculiar but somehow always turned out right. We trusted his marketing judgment completely.

If the politics are Byzantine in some publicly held corporations, they are positively Machiavellian in some private companies. At Adidas, Horst had to share the decision-making powers with his mother and his four sisters. There was a lot of competition in the family, and Horst told us up front, "If my mother and sisters think this is my idea, they're not going to go for it." He would then "coach" us on how best to sell the idea to the rest of his family.

When Horst decided that Adidas would design and manufacture the official tennis shoe for the Association of Tennis Professionals

(ATP), true to form, Horst knew his mother and sisters would fight this decision tooth and nail. He also knew that the only way to get them to go along was to make them feel that not only was this deal their idea, but that he was dead set against it. He had us tell his mother, "We're really having a hard time convincing Horst to do this ATP idea, Mrs. Dassler. This is a terrific opportunity for Adidas, but Horst is being very difficult. Can you help us?"

Horst was a brilliant manipulator. Sometimes he would use us with his family to accomplish his own internal agenda. But his overall vision was not only almost always right for Adidas, it was almost always right for us as well. So we didn't mind knowing we were being used every once in a while.

The Power of Secretaries

I have learned from experience that executive secretaries or administrative assistants of important corporate officials can be powerful allies. They are the sentries at the gate, and can be a big help not only in getting you through to their bosses, but in guiding you as to when the timing is most propitious for accomplishing your aims.

Executive secretaries can also be powerful enemies. They have reached their positions because they are extremely capable, but also because they are perceptive about people. Inured to false flattery and insincere compliments, they can spot a phony a mile away. Their power is sometimes such that if you get on their wrong side, you might as well forget your relationship with their boss.

My approach to the secretaries of important people is to let them know subtly that I am appreciative of their skills and their authority, and that I am aware that they are in the position they are in because they are excellent at their job.

For example, when I call I might say, "I'd like to speak to Mr. So-and-so, and he knows me, but can you tell me if this is a good time?" Right away you are letting the secretary know that she's more than a message taker. Not only are you acknowledging her position and authority, you're asking her for her judgment.

We try very hard to have more than perfunctory relationships with the secretaries of the leading people with whom we deal. We try always to know their names and treat them with courtesy and respect, and we endeavor to acknowledge special favors with a thank you note or card.

Recently, while in New York, I had some business at Sony's U.S. headquarters. While I was there, I stopped in at Mr. Morita's office to drop off a couple of tickets for his secretary for an upcoming tennis event, since I happened to know she loves tennis.

I declined her invitation to "poke my head in to say hello to Mr. Morita," but I know that when I really do need to get a message through to him, she will go out of her way to help me.

Dealing with
Corporate-Sized Egos

I once asked a doctor friend of mine why so many of his peers seemed to have such poor bedside manners. I was quite surprised by his answer. "It may be a matter of natural selection," he said. "The kinds of people who can get into medical school, get through it, and endure the process of becoming doctors are not the kind who have time for niceties. They are smart, arrogant, obsessive-compulsive people by nature, and the medical system encourages these traits. The very things that allow them to become doctors in the first place are what makes them difficult to deal with as people."

The same type of natural selection process seems to exist in corporations. By the time someone has survived the corporate wars and risen to the top of the ladder or to a position of authority, he or she invariably seems to possess certain traits—intelligence to be sure, but also the expectation of ego gratification from others.

The survivors of the corporate wars often get their identities from their positions. This is a very powerful factor. You sometimes have to deal with a "Don't-you-know-who-I-am?" attitude.

For instance, the rage today, started by Lee Iacocca of Chrysler, seems to be using your ad budget to make yourself famous on television. It's the age when Remington president, Victor Kiam, can go on TV and say, "I liked the company so much, I bought it."

What is the best way to deal with these oversized egos? It is simply understanding that playing up to and placating them is an absolute fact of business life. Take some solace in the fact that no one is exempt. Rather than being constantly angered by the ego-driven response, learn to accept it and deal with it.

Even a Donald Trump has to go into his deals prepared to eat some crow. If he tries to realign the West Side of Manhattan, he knows that he is going to be criticized and vilified for it and will have to placate hundreds of commissioners and committees just to move forward.

Rather than being surprised by this reaction, he expects it, remains flexible, and prepares for it by already having his contingency plans in place. Trump knows he only has two choices going in: He can take his model skyscrapers and go home, or he can deal with the problems as they come up. When dealing with corporations, you have to be prepared to run the same sort of gauntlet and take whatever certain egos are more than happy to dish out, just as you would with individuals.

ProServ has had combat training in dealing with outsized egos, as I'm sure most service organizations have. Our "boot camp," however, has been the experiences of dealing with sports federation officials all over the world. In working with amateur sports organizations, whether it's the Olympic organizing committees or tennis federations, the personalities of some officials are enough to make the egos found in corporations seem like shrinking violets. There is the expectation of enjoying all the corporate percs without the responsibility and accountability that usually accompanies the privileges. These officials consider themselves "unpaid volunteers," but if you looked at their lifestyles, you'd see that they fly all over the world in grand style with all their expenses fully paid. They fly the Concorde, ride in limousines, and stay in luxury hotel suites. Even though they tell you they work for nothing, they live like an Iacocca and expect to be treated the same way. Since their volunteer organizations don't have to make a profit, these officials don't even have to justify their actions on any economic basis, which makes them even more difficult to deal with.

The Art of Favors

One of the realities of dealing with the corporate world is that a lot of business is done on the basis of a subtle exchange of favors. It's the fine art of human relationships. Since I am involved in the sports entertainment industry, I am often in a position to do favors for people, whether it's taking a client to dinner with Michael Jordan or Jimmy Connors or getting someone tickets to a tennis tournament or getting their kids jobs as ball boys at a tennis event.

There is no doubt in my mind that doing favors for others in business is often going to benefit you later on. I have found that you must do these favors without any strings attached. If you even remotely convey the sense that you are creating an obligation, you sabotage all your efforts at goodwill. It's almost Zen-like: The more you think you are doing something to get someone obligated, the less likely it is going to turn out that way.

If I gave a corporate client two tickets to the U.S. Open and the next day was sitting with him in my box and said, "By the way, I need someone to buy a $100,000 TV spot," then it would be very obvious that my gift of the tickets was a not very subtle form of obligation.

On the other hand, it's only human nature that if you do something nice for someone, that person will usually remember it, if only subconsciously, and will make some effort to be accommodating later on. All else being exactly equal, that person's subconscious will make it 51–49. For this reason, whenever we're in a position to do someone a favor, I try to make it happen.

If you extend yourself on somebody's behalf you run the risk of having it backfire on you in some way, and a lot of people simply aren't willing to take that risk.

I disagree with that approach. ProServ has two boxes at the U.S. Open. One is right at courtside. The other is several rows back. You actually get a better view of the match from the box that is farther back and higher up. Every year, there are people who will say, "Gosh, maybe next year you can get me in the front box." Every year we have to contend with this, but in the long run the gesture of the tickets is what is ultimately remembered.

The true art of favors has very little to do with the favor itself. Rather, it is the care and consideration it conveys. There is probably no more powerful "currency" in business than conveying genuine care and concern.

Several years ago I flew to Atlanta to meet a ranking advertising executive for Coca-Cola—a man who has a considerable amount to say about Coke's television advertising budget.

I was looking forward to my first meeting with this very influential media buyer. When I arrived, I learned that the meeting had been canceled because his daughter had been rushed to the hospital with a serious illness earlier that morning.

Since I have two daughters of my own, I could empathize with the fear, panic, and the pain this person must have been experiencing. When I phoned my office, I asked my secretary to make sure to send flowers to the hospital, and I dictated a note to go with the flowers. Thereafter I totally forgot about it. Because I didn't know this person at all, I certainly didn't expect to hear from him. Several months later, I happened to call his office. This person picked up the phone. "I'm glad you called," he said, "because I wanted to thank you for the flowers. My daughter is fine." We spoke a little about our kids and then he said, "What were you calling about?" "Actually," I said, "I was trying to get Coke to buy a couple of commercial spots for a tournament we're televising." He said, "Call me back in thirty minutes." When I called back, he bought $60,000 worth of ad time.

Those flowers had cost about $35, but for this father I think they conveyed our care and concern, and that is priceless.

Remember a Person When He Is Down

We always try to send a card to anyone with whom we've done business who has been fired or squeezed out. This is done not only because we want to express our feeling for this person, but also because good people usually pop up again in other important positions.

The Corporate Client
Traps and Pitfalls

The innate differences—from size to structure from attitude to outlook—that often exist between the "mother ship" corporation and her hundreds of outside suppliers can create a whole host of traps and pitfalls for the unwary small corporate-dependent service company.

There is a tendency, for instance, to view the large cash-rich corporation as the "have" and oneself as the "have not." Most can see the distinction, but need to be aware of the inherent traps and pitfalls it engenders.

The "We Aim to Please" Trap

In your desire to keep the corporate client happy and to build the relationship, there is sometimes an overwhelming temptation to take on assignments that are outside your expertise.

What often happens is that once you do something well for a client, both you and the client want to expand the relationship, and the client will come back to you with "an opportunity" that is only tangentially related to your expertise. In the client's mind, this new job is a natural extension of the relationship, but you know you're going to have to staff up in a totally different, unfamiliar, and perhaps unprofitable way. The temptation to accept the new opportunity anyway is overwhelming, but you must resist.

We have packaged and televised literally hundreds of tennis tournaments. In this area, I would put our expertise up against anyone, including the networks. One of our corporate clients once asked us if we could put together a regional basketball or football package that they would be interested in sponsoring. The temptation to do so was great, but we declined to get involved. Football is one of the most difficult sports to televise. At the time, our television division wasn't seasoned enough or established enough to take on that kind of assignment, even though, from the client's perspective, it seemed a natural extension of what we were already doing for them. Of course, if we had taken the project on and failed, we could have also hurt ourselves worse, by jeopardizing the good relationship we had already established with this client.

Don't Act Against Your Best Instincts

Closely related to the above is a willingness to do something against your own best instincts simply to please the client. Don't give in to this temptation, because invariably the results are against everyone's best interests. What the client is buying is your expertise, and when you go against your own expertise, not only are you letting the client down, you are going to get the blame when things don't work out well.

Recently Paine Webber asked us to move a tournament they were sponsoring, the Paine Webber Classic in Orlando, Florida, to Palm Beach. The path of least resistance would have been just to accommodate them. We knew, however, that if we went from a big city like Orlando to a small one like Palm Beach, it would jeopardize the very existence of the tournament. With a population close to a million people, Orlando was a better market for the public and the press.

As much as we hated to lose Paine Webber, we kept the tournament in Orlando and found another sponsor.

The "Big Companies Mean Big Deals" Trap

Anyone who has large corporations as clients has at some point thought, "Could this be the gold mine at the end of the dusty trail? Could this be my home run?" You fantasize to yourself, "If this company earns eleven billion dollars a year, why can't I have a couple of million?" That is exactly the attitude that kills so many relationships, because companies are very sensitive to this type of thinking.

Don't think that just because a company is big you should be charging bigger fees. In truth, the larger the company, the more fragmented it is, and the more people there are to approve any substantial expenditure.

If you really want to do business with a giant, or any company for that matter, the best plan is to start slowly and develop a relationship. After doing a series of small projects and building mutual trust, you can then seek the larger projects with substantial sums at stake.

While "pushing" can do some good, I believe that for the most part, the relationship with a corporate client must be allowed to grow naturally and logically. Over the years we have had a good relationship with Marvin Koslow of Bristol Myers, makers of Bufferin, Vitalis, Clairol, and a number of other major products. Bristol Myers is one of the biggest consumer advertisers in the country, and Marvin Koslow is one of the most powerful people in the advertising business.

At the 1987 U.S. Open, Marvin approached me and asked me to introduce him to Arthur Ashe. "I have a little idea I want to talk to him about," he said. What Koslow didn't tell me was that in six months time, studies showing the benefits of aspirin in preventing heart attacks (especially in previous heart attack victims) would be made public. Since Arthur had survived a heart attack and had had two bypass operations and was now in good health, Bristol Myers figured he would be a perfect spokesman for Bufferin.

The new Bufferin commercial, starring Ashe, had already been produced the day the aspirin news broke. Koslow later told me it was the biggest one-day media buy for one TV commercial in Bristol Myers's history.

Arthur, of course, was a perfect choice, but who knows if this deal ever would have been made if we hadn't already had the ongoing, friendly relationship with Marvin Koslow and Bristol Myers?

To start small with companies, make sure you have a *"start small plan"* in place to offer them. To help companies get their feet wet we have in recent years begun to produce the official programs for the tournaments we run. These programs are marginally profitable, but it's a good way to involve companies in sports for the first time. It's much more acceptable for an advertising agency to calculate the value of an ad in a program than it is to assess the value of becoming an official sponsor of an event. The company sees it as an advertising buy which they are accustomed to analyzing, rather than an "image buy." Once we get the company involved in sports, it becomes much easier to expand that relationship later on—putting one of our clients into their ads, for instance—than it would be if we had to start from scratch.

The "New Money Spends Better than Old" Trap

Another danger when going after corporate clients is ignoring your current clients while going after the new ones. Familiarity breeds complacency. The clients you don't have can sometimes seem more attractive than the ones you do have, simply because the grass is always greener. Whenever you take your clients for granted, inevitably the competition reappears from nowhere.

The "Not Invented Here" Trap

One of the major problems of selling to any company—and advertising agencies especially will attest to this—is that companies are most enamored with their own ideas. The way to get around that is to do everything you can to factor the company's own thinking into your presentation.

Jay Chiat, the chairman of Chiat/Day (the hottest ad agency in the country over the past few years), does something as a matter of course which is practically revolutionary in his industry. He includes the client during the initial creative sessions to help formulate the advertising campaign. From the client's standpoint, the "dog-and-pony" shows are never that far off the mark because the company itself has had some input. When the client applauds the official presentation down the road, part of what he or she is applauding is the client's own concept.

Another friend of mine in the advertising business was hired as a consultant to help create a new ad campaign. The problem, he saw, was in the headline, and in one of those rare moments of inspiration, it occurred to him almost instantly what the new headline should be. Wisely, he held his tongue.

If he had blurted it out on the spot it could have looked too easy. He also ran the risk of having it rejected because "How could anything that quick be right?" Instead, he asked the clients to let him work on it for a couple of weeks. When he presented his new headline two and a half weeks later, they were not only thrilled but more than happy to pay him a substantial fee.

The point is that it took years and a considerable amount of experience for my friend to get where he could "flash" on a solution quickly, but clients tend to discount that factor. If they get results too quickly, often they wonder how difficult or skillful the solution really was.

There is absolutely no benefit in making your efforts look too easy. In the long run, people would much rather pay for blood, sweat, and tears than immediate inspiration.

Take Advantage of Your Built-in Strengths

If it generally does not work to leap into major deals and it is dangerous to get into areas where your expertise or capabilities will be sorely tested, then how do you extend or build on an existing corporate relationship? What you must remember is that as a small outside service organization, you have distinct natural advantages over the corporation itself, namely speed, flexibility, and decisiveness. Over the years we have tried to use these qualities to our best advantage.

When David Foster was chairman of Colgate, for instance, we met with him to sell him on the idea of having Colgate become the title sponsor for the Men's Grand Prix tennis circuit, a multimillion-dollar commitment. He was somewhat receptive, but had some additional thoughts about our proposal and what he wanted to accomplish on behalf of Colgate.

When we left our meeting with him, we returned directly to the hotel room and began revising our proposal to his specifications. We even aroused a typist in the middle of the night to type it up in final form. When David arrived at work the next morning, the almost totally revised proposal, incorporating all his suggestions, was already on his desk. Needless to say, he was impressed. Several days later, when we closed the whole deal, it was clear that the speed with which we had acted was still on his mind. We had been able to do in one evening what would have taken his company three weeks.

Speed and decisiveness together can be a potent combination. We once flew to Cincinnati to finalize what had been a very long and arduous negotiation with Charlie Mechem, then chairman of Taft Broadcasting. Taft had agreed to construct a tennis facility that would serve as the permanent home of the ATP Championships. It was a complex deal and every time we met, the deal kept changing.

I began to feel that unless we closed this deal soon, there was the possibility it might not get done at all. I said to David Falk, who had flown out with me, "We need to get this thing signed today."

During the meeting, Mechem, who is one of the most charming and smartest men we deal with, and I battled back and forth on the intricate parts of the deal. The terms kept constantly changing. The whole time David was scribbling like crazy on a yellow legal pad.

When all the details were finally agreed upon, I said, "Okay, David, let's get this thing written up and back to Charlie as soon as we can." David, who is a lawyer, handed me six sheets of yellow pages from his pad. "Is this soon enough?" he said. I looked at the pages, then handed them to Mechem, and said, "Well, Charlie, here it is. Please read it and sign it."

To Charlie's credit, he read through it once and signed it on the spot.

After the meeting I asked David, "How did you get that agreement written so fast?" "We didn't have a choice," he said. "The way things were going, I knew if we didn't walk out of there with a signed agreement, it would be a different deal by tomorrow."

The Kind of
Clients You Really Want

Over the years we've had every sort of corporate client relationship imaginable—good, bad, long, short, close, distant, successful, failed. As a result, I think we have developed a pretty good sense of the kind of corporate client you ideally would want to have.

First, the more personal the relationship, the better it is going to be for both sides. People such as Bjorn Ahlstrom, Rick Dowden, Don Marron, Michael Fuchs, Kay Koplowitz, George Ball, Marv Koslow, Bill Grimes, and Ken Schanzer have become close personal friends, and in each case I'm sure there were times, were it not for these friendships, our corporate relationships would have otherwise been sorely tested. The same seems to hold true at all levels of our company: When there is a personal relationship between one of us and our corporate counterpart, there invariably seems to be a smoother working relationship.

Second, in the best of all corporate worlds, you would like to feel your client is fair-minded and considerate. We've never had Warner Communications as a client, but I've heard they have a rule that all small suppliers get paid in less than ten days. Rather than take care of their major suppliers first, Warner's tries to accommodate the little guys where cash flow is obviously more important. This is the opposite of what most major corporations do. If this is true, that alone would tell you volumes about doing business with Warner's.

Basic courtesy and politeness is also a big plus. I remember a comment one of my colleagues once made about Charlie Mechem, whom I described earlier. Although he was a very tough negotiator, Mechem had such style and grace and such a polite way about him that once, after he had bested us in a negotiation, my associate said, "He just killed us, but he really made you feel good in the process. I was sort of happy for him."

Last, and perhaps most important, the best corporate-client relationships seem to have all the markings of a true partnership. There is mutual concern, mutual consideration, and a feeling pervading the relationship that two heads are better than one.

One of the best clients our television division has ever developed is Anheuser-Busch, makers of Budweiser, Busch beer, Michelob, and a number of other world-famous brands. Anheuser-Busch is all-powerful in the world of television sports. What is so effective about their power is that they never use it. You know it's there, but the Anheuser-Busch executives go out of their way to treat you as someone they need, rather than the other way around.

To give you one example, when Anheuser-Busch is your client, every December is like the twelve days of Christmas. Some emissary from the company shows up every day with a different gift, culminating on New Year's Eve when a truck from the local distributor pulls up and wheels up three cases of Michelob to your front door.

More important is the way they treat you in a business setting. If you take them a proposal, they may give you a decision on it before you leave the office. They try to figure out ways to make something happen rather than to make it not happen. As a consequence, everybody in the world of sports wants to deal with Anheuser-Busch. They are the biggest gorilla in the forest, but they treat everyone so nicely they always get the best bananas.

If we've ever had a problem with Anheuser-Busch, it might be that they are too accommodating, almost too willing to listen to anyone who has something to say.

I will never forget the time Bob Briner and I flew to New York to meet with Jerry Solomon, who has a major say in how Anheuser-Busch spends its $150 million in sports television advertising every year. We were trying to convince Jerry to sponsor a TV bowling series, which our television company would produce, pitting ordinary amateur bowlers against one another in a nationally televised playoff. Jerry was against the idea of using local bowlers. He felt the game's stars were needed to attract more viewers.

"Bowling gets good TV ratings," we argued, "because it is a sport that lends itself very well to being televised, and fans tune in because they like to watch bowling, not because they know who the stars are."

Solomon was not at all convinced. We were deep into this friendly but intense discussion when Jerry's regular shoeshine man came into his office and began shining his shoes. When he finished, Jerry graciously motioned him over to shine our shoes as well. Meanwhile, we continued to argue, and the shoeshine man continued to polish and buff. But then a voice popped up from beneath my knee. "You know, I'm going to have to go along with Jerry on this one." The guy shining my shoes then proceeded to present a fairly cogent argument for Solomon's point of view in this discussion.

Both of us were so taken aback that we couldn't press our position any further, and soon left licking our wounds. As we left the building and walked out onto Madison Avenue, I turned to Briner and said, "Can you believe that? Shot down by the shoeshine boy!"

CHAPTER EIGHT

GROWING

Growth—specifically how to expand and at what rate—is a significant subject for any personal service business. The old adage that "you either get bigger or you get smaller" certainly applies to the personal service field. If you grow too fast or if you fail to provide the proper infrastructure, the "personal" is likely to become impersonal, and then you are through.

Of course, the problem of growing too fast is the kind of "problem" that anyone who is not yet fully established would love to have. For most start-up client businesses, survival is a more pressing concern.

Unlike product companies where there is an income base to build on each year, most new service businesses are only as solvent as their last client. Old business ends, new business begins, and the struggle involves simply maintaining the status quo—keeping one's head above water.

How do you break out of this linear "growth" pattern? How do you get to the point where your business takes on its own momentum? How do you achieve the desired state of spending most of your time servicing (and retaining) your present clients rather than chasing after the new ones?

The key is referrals and reputation. This is the flashpoint of growth in any client business, the point when most of the potential new clients who walk in your front door are already convinced you are the person for them.

Goodwill

In any business that deals in intangibles, there is no substitute for goodwill. By goodwill, I mean reputation, using the job you have done for others in the past to create a residue of good feelings about yourself and the services you provide.

Because Arthur Ashe and Stan Smith were so well known, it was fairly easy for us to attract other major names on the tennis circuit in the beginning. By the early seventies we represented most of the top American players including Harold Solomon, Bob Lutz, Brian Gottfried, Dick Stockton, Tom Gorman, Marty Riessen, and Dennis Ralston.

By 1972, our business hit its first plateau. Tennis was going great guns, but we were starting to get caught on the client treadmill. We were signing up the new, hot young tennis stars just as our old pros were about to wind down.

During this time, Arthur Ashe was asked to be the guest speaker at the Women's Democratic Club in Washington before four hundred people. His father and I went along with him. During his speech, Arthur stated, "I am especially pleased to be here today with the two people whom I trust the most in my life. In fact, I would trust either of them with my life. One of them is my father, the other is my lawyer, Donald Dell."

Two days later, a woman who had attended that luncheon called me on the phone. She asked for a copy of Arthur's speech, which I sent to her. She turned out to be the mother of Notre Dame basketball star Collis Jones, who was about to graduate. Mrs. Jones was looking for someone to represent her son, and because of Arthur's speech, she chose me. Just like that, we were into basketball representation.

It was imperative for us to do a good job for Collis Jones because our performance would establish our reputation in the world of basketball. In fact, we did such a good job for him that we were able to get a strong foothold at Notre Dame, which eventually helped us in signing other Notre Dame stars such as Adrian Dantley. Even more important, it gave us a toehold in college basketball, which today is almost as big a profit center for us as tennis.

When it comes right down to it, the only way you build a client list is through your reputation. The first step to building a reputation is understanding the reputation you want to have *from the client's point of view.*

For instance, many law firms believe that the best word of mouth they could have is for people to say, "They may be real sons of bitches, but I want them to be my sons of bitches." If you are ever in the position to be one of their clients, you might well want someone that tough to defend you. This sort of reasoning is particularly apparent in divorce cases. Marvin Mitchelson's reputation cuts both ways: One, it attracts clients, and two, when a man finds out his ex-mate is being represented by Mitchelson, he is more likely to settle.

I believe a version of this applies to almost any service profession. A newcomer to the catering business, for instance, is probably better off establishing a reputation for being casual, hip, maybe even trendy than trying to compete head on with the established formal caterers.

Reputations, of course, are built on different criteria in different professions. The reputation you want to have may also change as your business evolves. For instance, our reputation is now built primarily on the fact that we maximize income for our clients. When we first went into pro basketball, it was such a shady jungle, we figured out that if we wanted to establish a reputation quickly, we would have to set ourselves apart in terms of honesty and integrity. Just by dealing straightforwardly with the coaches and players and parents, we began to stand out!

Obviously, the reputation you want to have precede you is the one that best serves your particular interests at each stage of growth in your company. Most new companies, for instance, place a premium on being perceived as hungry and aggressive. Growing companies try to reach out with a "come grow with us" message. Older established companies stress experience, contacts, maturity, and longevity.

Reputation is so important in the growth of any client-dependent business, you really can't give too much thought to how you want to be perceived and what most aptly fits the realities of your company.

Getting the Word Out—Referrals

In order to have your reputation precede you, you obviously need someone to get the word out for you—someone (other than yourself) to toot your horn. The two most obvious sources are the satisfied clients themselves and those who are close to these clients.

Although our reputation first was well established in tennis, we were unknowns in the world of basketball. As new guys on the block, we were starting from a disadvantage. We began to work very hard at getting close to the influential college coaches—not just the best coaches, but those who had a reputation for being very close to and

respected by their players. It was important that they knew not only
the job we had done for Collis but for our tennis clients as well, since
negotiating skills are obviously transferable from one sport to the
other.

For any service business to grow, it's essential to build a network
of missionaries. In the legal profession, referrals are everything. In
the medical profession, referrals are how most people find their way
to specialists. In our business, it's our *life blood:* We had to cultivate
the coaches if we were to get the word out. Once we began to make
an impression at that level, our basketball business took off.

We have never tried to convince coaches to say, "You should go
with ProServ." All we have ever asked is that they judge us on our
reputation, our integrity, and our track record, and if we pass muster
on all of these counts, then give us a full and equal opportunity along
with others.

In fact, this is how we signed Michael Jordan. By the time Michael
left the University of North Carolina at the end of his junior year,
I had known his basketball coach, Dean Smith, for fifteen years, and
we had represented twenty of his top players. Our competitors said,
"Forget Michael Jordan. ProServ has an inside track with Coach
Smith." And we did have, to the extent that we were among three
representatives he recommended to Michael.

But how could Dean have done otherwise? He had seen the job
we had done for his former players for almost fifteen years. If consistency and track record count for anything, then Dean Smith felt
confident and comfortable recommending us.

If there's a catch, it's that you can't fake it. You really do have
to deliver. It would have been a far tougher feat to fool Coach Smith
for fifteen years than it was to deliver for his Carolina players. When
you do a good job, don't be shy about getting the word out.

The payoff is getting calls from potential clients that begin, "So-
and-so recommended that I get in touch . . ." That's when you know

your business is no longer a year-to-year or month-to-month proposition.

Staffing Up

At the end of the day, reputation is built primarily on *performance*. Just as a good reputation can do worlds of good for your business, a bad reputation can kill it just as quickly.

Every time you have a disappointed or disenchanted client, you've made an emissary for negative word of mouth. As I mentioned earlier, one of the quickest ways to embitter a client is to make the client feel that you don't have enough time for him or her.

This lapse in good client relations involves the whole issue of staffing up, of having the right support staff in place so that you are not only bringing in new clients part of the time, but you're also giving them the first-class service they deserve.

I wish I could say we've always anticipated our needs and always proceeded smoothly from one plateau to the next as we grew. Of course, it never works that way. Usually, the staff ends up doubling and tripling its responsibilities until you're bursting at the seams. Finally you realize you need to get some additional people. By the way, it's important that you never let the client be aware that you are going through an up-against-the-wall period. I constantly tell our staff, "We're handling these people's lives, so don't let them see our own lives in disarray."

The strength of the infrastructure of any business obviously depends on the people you hire. In any service or client business that's just about all you've got—the brainpower and personalities of the people working for you.

When we go through one of our periodic expansion phases, we look to hire people with good "people skills" first. People who know how to handle other people can make bad news sound okay, whereas people who don't can take the best news and make it sound like a disaster. I happen to believe that most "people skills" are something that can't be taught, or if they can be, it occurs at a much earlier time in people's lives. We can teach people how to manage clients, but how good they will be ultimately depends on what they themselves bring to the party.

Secondly, I want to hire people whose strengths are my weaknesses. I know, for instance, that I tend to get impatient too easily, so most of our client managers are very patient and understanding people. Finance is something else that has never been a strong point of mine, so we had to pay particular attention to getting the best financial advisors around.

Finally, once the right people are in place, give them something to do. The key to growth of any client business is to delegate, delegate, delegate.

Delegation

There are three enormous obstacles to effective delegation. The first is that if you have confidence in your own abilities, part of *you* believes you can do everything better than everyone else—even if this belief is constantly being undermined by the facts. If, in defiance of all good sense, you choose to believe this anyway, you're always going to be the one person doing everything, which is fine, as long as you are content to stay the same size (in which case you will have an altogether different concern: how not to stagnate).

The second problem is that most of us, under the time pressures of business, are not good teachers. Since most people who have their own business have gone through the stage of having to do everything for themselves, there is a built-in reluctance to commit to the time and patience it takes to train others. Of course you have to. You have to invest the ten hours it takes to train someone to do something you could have done in ten minutes, because those ten hours will save you hundreds of hours later on.

The third difficulty is susceptibility to flattery. There is always a tendency for clients to want to deal with the top person. This is particularly true in personal service businesses. You know prospective clients are thinking, "If he's the leader, he must be the best man." Although it may be ego-gratifying to be thought of in this vein, it's not very gratifying to watch your business go down the tubes.

Even if you're prepared to give up the glory, what about the clients? They may still want to deal with the head of the company. The solution is to introduce the clients' personal contact at the very first meeting. Clients then perceive the two of you as being their "team." Later on, when your clients are directed to your associate, they won't feel as if they're being shoved down the ladder.

Is this a "dirty trick" to play on clients? In fact, it is just the opposite. You know there are people within your organization who will be better equipped to deal with the clients' problems and will also be more responsive to their needs, which is something clients will quickly catch on to themselves. In the beginning it may take some convincing, and the best convincing you can do is to bring in the client's contact at that very first meeting.

Corporate Cultures

What intrigues me about management styles and corporate cultures is that hard evidence suggests that both positive and negative motivation have their strong points. What is less clear is the optimum mix of the two. There are many companies with an internal culture of "measuring up"—are you good enough to work here? Who's to say this is the wrong approach?

There are many law firms, for instance, where the whole ethic consists of how many billable hours you have charged. If you want to become a partner, you must prove through your actions that you are totally dedicated and love nothing more than to come into the office on Sundays and work on cases. It may not be particularly healthy, but it seems to work.

I would feel uncomfortable motivating our people by creating a do-you-measure-up climate or making them feel they have to prove themselves by committing to an unbalanced lifestyle.

Early in my career I was fortunate to be exposed to the Kennedy mystique. Part of that mystique was the feeling one got from being accepted by the Kennedy clan. As one of Bobby Kennedy's advance men, I was made to feel that I was someone special, that I was doing important things. All the Kennedys had the knack of creating an environment you felt privileged to be a part of. Working for Sargent Shriver at the Office for Economic Opportunity was very much the same experience. Sargent Shriver is a hero of mine because he is extremely idealistic, sympathetic, and charismatic. He is so upbeat that just being around him has always been uplifting. I would do anything for that man.

Our staff at OEO met every morning at 9 A.M. Sarge called us the "Nine O'Clock Commandos," and issued us plastic membership cards that listed the "rights and privileges."

1. Seven-day weeks.

2. Fourteen-hour days.

3. Telephone calls at all times and all places.

4. Impossible assignments to do by yesterday.

5. An unforgettable experience in dedication, participation, and accomplishment.

Some may think this was a little corny, but it really did embody the spirit of our organization.

In working for Bobby Kennedy and Sargent Shriver, and also getting to know Ethel Kennedy and Eunice Kennedy Shriver as a result, I came to appreciate the importance of family and the role that it plays in running any corporation.

I must add here that not only is it important for people in the firm to feel they are a part of a family, it is equally important for your family to have a feeling they are a part of the firm. I know this goes against a lot of pop psychology which says you should leave your work at five o'clock, go home, and devote yourself entirely to your family. Well, this may be okay for other businesses, but it will, in my opinion, never work in client management.

My wife, Carole, who is not on the ProServ payroll and has no official position in the company, is one of the most important assets of the firm. She is a very trusted advisor. I value her instincts on many aspects of the business. She is also very much involved in client recruiting, especially when we entertain in our home. Also, she maintains a close friendship with many clients and their spouses, which is of enormous help. Carole is an integral part of the success of ProServ.

Perhaps it is possible to be a success in the client-management business without active involvement of your spouse, but I am sure it is much more difficult.

That to me is the corporate culture I have tried to create at ProServ, the feeling of belonging to a family unit with strong loyalties, and getting the job done, somehow. This is a particularly appropriate corporate culture for today, because with the loss of the extended family, people look to their jobs to take up some of the slack. Unfortunately, in the wake of all the recent corporate acquisitions and mergers, the larger companies are moving away from this feeling that your work really *matters,* that your work makes an important *contribution* to the team. For a small- or medium-sized company, I think this makes the family corporate culture even more appealing. It is what your company can offer that the mega-companies no longer can.

It Comes from the Top

One of our senior people once said to me, "We demand too much from our employees. They aren't owners and yet we still expect them to work as if they were."

"Wait a minute," I said. "Why shouldn't they? They have terrific, challenging jobs; they're well paid, and who in here doesn't work long hours? You and I sure as hell do."

What hit me at that point is how the entire corporate culture is often set by one person—the person at the top. I suppose that is pretty obvious, but the point is that when you are the head of your company, every action you take (or don't take) has ramifications well beyond what you may realize.

Like Sargent Shriver at the OEO, you set the style, the tone, and the level of commitment for your entire company.

What this means is that you can demand a great deal from your employees, and you will be constantly amazed at the results, as long as you are equally (or even more) demanding of yourself. If there were ever a situation where *actions* speak louder than words, it is with the top person in a small company.

The converse also holds true. If you demand or expect more from your employees than from yourself, then your credibility will be totally shot across the board.

Sellers Versus Servicers

In any service organization, there are the selling people who hustle the new business and bring in the dollars, and there are the servicing

people who service the accounts. In service companies, there is sometimes a tendency to devalue the jobs of the service personnel, not
because they are any less valuable, but because their value is tougher
to measure in tangible terms.

Sellers are generally compensated in direct proportion to the income they bring in, based on a formula that is generally agreed upon
beforehand. With service personnel the scorecard is less concrete.
The *quality* of the service you provide is obviously crucial to the
ongoing success of any service business. That's self-evident. Your
employment and salary policies must reflect this reality.

Odds and Ends

In setting up a client business there are always policies which have
to be established and decisions which have to be made relating to
overhead and expenses. Two of the most important are the decisions
you make relating to the appearances you present to prospective
clients and the fees you decide to charge them.

The Way You Look

The funny thing about the impression created by your office—its
size, locale, and decor—is that everyone knows that the idea is to
create an image of success regardless of reality. Yet everyone buys
into the same deception. The way your office looks may be the one
issue in business where *form* has the edge over *substance*. Who hasn't
walked into someone's office for the first time and thought, "I bet
these people think I'm going to be impressed by this impressive-
looking office"? And amazingly, you are always impressed anyway!

By "looking impressive" I don't mean you need Impressionist
paintings or the latest designer fabrics on your walls. It's worse to

have your offices look *overdone* than underdone. If the look is contrived, then your office loses its capacity to impress.

Two rooms must look good. First is the reception area. It is obviously the first space that everyone sees. It should be clean and uncluttered, a pleasant work space (as opposed to an airport lounge) or something resembling your den at home.

I also believe there is nothing more important than having a good conference room. You can get away with having less than stellar individual offices, but you must make the conference room look attractive. If you say, "We're meeting in the conference room," you make the meeting seem more important. And you never have to show the client your tiny office. The conference room also has its practical uses. If things have to be spread out, this is the place to do it. I would go so far as to say that even if you have a three-room office, one should be a conference room.

The Way You Sound

The importance of the first contact with a client can't be overstated, and, therefore, you must make sure that the person who answers your telephone has a good phone manner, and answers by the third ring. Although it is helpful if the person answering your phone is fully conversant about your services—what they are and who in your organization is best equipped to answer the caller's questions—what is said is not as important as *how* it's said. If you are agitated or irritated and you call a company and you hear a friendly, sympathetic voice on the other end of the line, your vitriol is half-spent by the time you reach the person with whom you are displeased.

As for being put "on hold," most people understand that this is inevitable sometimes. What drives people crazy is being put on hold indefinitely. After a few moments the caller should be given a choice: "Would you prefer to hold or can I take a message or have someone call you back?"

I am appalled at the phone manners of many employees whose companies should know better. Even when starting out, have a written phone policy—how you want the phone answered, how long to ask people to hold, and so on. In many cases the people answering the phones simply don't know proper phone procedures and need only to be shown in order to practice good phone manners.

Fees

There's an old Chinese proverb that states, "The wise dentist collects his fee while the tooth is still hurting." Unfortunately, there is still much truth to this adage.

In our business the money comes to us, and we make the disbursements to the clients. I prefer this for several reasons, the obvious one being that we get paid. It also means we rarely have to raise the issue of fees and commissions with our clients. I also want the client to cash or deposit a ProServ check. It sends a subliminal message about our success on the client's behalf.

But not all service businesses work this way. If you have any doubt about getting paid or if your client is only semisolvent, then you have to have the courage to address this issue up front, even at the risk of offending the client. After all, you're in business to get paid.

I have often seen lawyers penalized for their own success. Once they succeed on the client's behalf, the client begins to rationalize, "Well, he didn't have to do that much." The client factors in a time or value quotient and throws out the prearranged fee conversation. On those rare occasions when we work on a flat fee, rather than a commission basis, I believe in reasonable, up-front retainers.

Which brings up another point: Get the understanding in writing. Even though you and your client have a mutual trust, there is still good reason to put everything in writing. It protects you should a "worst-case" scenario arise. Written contracts serve as great memory joggers—an outline of your working relationship. If there's ever a misunderstanding, there's a piece of paper you can turn to.

What to charge a client varies from industry to industry and region to region. The only constant is that you have to be consistent. This obviously doesn't mean you have to charge everyone the same fee or percentage: What we charge a superstar athlete earning ten million dollars a year may be different from what we charge a kid who has yet to win a tournament and for whom we're going to have to work a lot harder. What's important is that you maintain consistency about your fee structure.

You should also assume that there are no secrets. Assume that every client you represent knows everything you are doing for every other client and what your agreements are with each of those clients. To save yourself embarrassment (or worse), be consistent.

Where fees are concerned, there is also tremendous power of precedent. A number of years ago, the fact that we refused to take a fee for our services on Moses Malone's first contract (because of the extenuating circumstances I mentioned earlier) made its way into *Sports Illustrated.* Several years later, when we signed up tennis player Tom Okker, it came time to discuss our commission structure, and he said facetiously, "Wait a minute, I want the same deal you gave to Moses Malone!"

Confidentiality

As far as I'm concerned, all client relationships are based on the same confidentiality rules that exist for doctors and lawyers and their patients and clients. Next to outright stealing or lying, the worst client-business sin is breaching a confidence. It's a case where the punishment almost always fits the crime because a breach of confidence almost always comes back to haunt you. Many a major client has been lost as a result of several indiscreet remarks.

The Competition

Competition obviously has an effect on the health and the size of your business for all sorts of reasons. There are many businesses—certain consulting fields, for instance—where the field is already so crowded the last thing that is needed is another consultant.

This has never been our problem. Sports management and marketing is a terribly difficult industry to break into, but once you get a foothold, the intense competition that exists within the industry can be quite healthy. I actually think the competition has been good for our business. It has kept us alert and vigilant. When the competition is always nipping at your heels, it inspires you to work harder.

Practically since we've been in business our biggest competitor has been International Management Group (IMG). In the field of tennis management, a small industry, ProServ and IMG are like Coke and Pepsi, Avis and Hertz. We have competed head-to-head against each other in every facet of tennis, basketball, and football all over the world. What is interesting about our relationship with IMG is that in addition to keeping us both hungry and competitive, it has made us more appreciative of each other's triumphs.

Despite the incessant competition between us, there is almost something good-natured about it. I make it a point to have breakfast with IMG's chairman, Mark McCormack, now and then. We may get together at the French Open or at Wimbledon and trade war stories. Given the intensity of our rivalry, I would have to say we are friendly competitors. Still, our companies love to one-up each other.

Several years ago I had gone to Dallas ostensibly to attend a tennis awards banquet. The real reason for my visit was to sign up Billy Scanlon, the number-one college player in the country at that time.

Shortly after arriving, I ran into Bud Stanner, who then was heading IMG's tennis division. Like me, Bud had come down to recruit Scanlon and was using the banquet as his cover.

That evening at the banquet, I was just leaving the men's room as Bud Stanner was walking in. We stopped and exchanged pleasantries, asked each other how things were going, and so on. As I started for the door, Stanner said, "Oh, by the way, we just signed Billy Scanlon today."

I could not allow Stanner to see my expression, but my whole body sagged. Scanlon was the major reason I had gone to Dallas, and IMG had aced us out. It was just like Stanner to rub it in in this matter-of-fact way. Stanner was so convincing and so casual that I dropped our chase on the spot, and I never got back to the Scanlon family again.

About a month later, I got a note from Scanlon's father saying that Billy had signed with IMG earlier that week! I had been totally had. To this day, Stanner never misses an opportunity to remind me.

On the other side of the scorecard, several years ago American sixteen-year-old tennis star Aaron Krickstein was seen as the next great hope for U.S. tennis, and there was a very strong competition for his affections among sports management companies. As always, the most intense competition was between ProServ and IMG.

For a time, IMG was certainly in the driver's seat with Aaron. But knowing that Aaron would be playing in the Israeli Open and that his entire family would be there to watch him, I came up with a plan. I sent my brother, Dick (who had recently returned from the pro circuit and was now working for us), to Tel Aviv completely unannounced, to see Aaron play. Aaron and his father were so impressed that Dick had flown all the way to Tel Aviv just to be with them and to support Aaron in the tournament, that Dr. Krickstein asked Dick to take Aaron under his wing that week and to show him some of the ropes of tour life.

During this time, Dick happened to be up in the Kricksteins' hotel suite one day when the phone rang. Dick picked it up and on the other end of the line was Bob Kain, IMG's director of tennis, calling to check up on his prize recruit. Kain immediately recognized Dick's voice and blurted out, "What the hell is going on over there?"

"Oh, nothing much," Dick said.

A few months later Aaron Krickstein decided to leave IMG and became a ProServ client.

Learning to Act in
Your Own Best Interest

A large contributor to growth in any personal service business is "personal growth" or the maturation of one's own skills in dealing with other people.

In the business of hitting tennis balls, there is no better example of "personal growth" than Jimmy Connors, who emerged on the tennis scene as a cocky young kid, but today has matured into one of the game's more gracious and likable players.

In the business of representing professional athletes, personal growth is not always so clear-cut or uncomplicated. For me, one of the most difficult forms of personal growth has been learning to act in my own best interest.

It's important not to let your own ego get in the way of what you really want to do or accomplish. I see this problem all the time in business: A valued employee is allowed to leave because the employer's ego will not allow him to make the appropriate placating gesture; or a business conflict becomes a disaster when both parties become so ego-bound neither can make the necessary accommodations.

This "ego entrenchment" is something I try to improve, and while I'm far from where I'd like to be, every once in a while something happens that convinces me I am making some progress.

In 1987, for instance, Joseph F. Cullman, former chairman of Phillip Morris and current chairman of the International Tennis Hall of Fame, approached me about serving a one-year term as its president. I was flattered by the offer but warned Joe and members of the nominating committee that I would be a very controversial choice. The International Tennis Hall of Fame represents the "establishment" side of tennis and, as a lawyer/manager and someone closely affiliated with the commercial side of the sport, I said, "Some of the old guard may see this as inviting the fox into the chicken coop."

That, as it turned out, was putting it mildly. When my name was placed in nomination before the membership, two of the members literally got up and walked out. Another member, a former president of the USTA, stood up and announced: "I am so opposed to this slate of nominees that if it is accepted by this membership I will resign." Even the outgoing president, who was sitting right next to me on the dais, felt compelled to speak up.

"If this slate were allowed to pass," he said, "it would be a sad day for the game of tennis."

As I sat there and listened to these "objections," my blood began to boil. Twenty years ago I would have said "the hell with them" and withdrawn my name from consideration. Ten years ago I might have left it in, but may have wanted to "get even" with my most vocal critics.

I decided instead that I really wanted the position for several reasons. Not only was it an honor and an important job, but I felt that through my corporate contacts and fund-raising skills, I could do a good job for the Hall of Fame. Also, I could give something back to the sport I loved. "Not only am I going to accept this position," I thought to myself, "I'm going to make everyone in this room *want* to work with me."

There was only one slate of candidates, and as a result, my nomination easily passed a vote of the full two hundred members. Before anyone could leave the room, however, I made a point of going around to my most vocal detractors, shaking their hands and saying to each of them something to the effect of "I'm really sorry you feel the way you do, but I hope my performance over the next year will change your mind."

My term as president of the International Tennis Hall of Fame has been both productive and pleasurable. And maybe that's what "personal growth" means—learning that sometimes it's better to accommodate people, even critics, than to steamroll over them. The second year I was reelected president of the International Tennis Hall of Fame by acclamation.

EPILOGUE

While becoming a "published author" has obviously been an immensely gratifying experience, it has been a frustrating—even humbling—one as well. I am now convinced that no matter how many times you might revise a manuscript it can never be the "perfect book" envisioned in your mind's eye. Moreover, when the book happens to be a collection of your best business advice you can't help becoming more aware of your own business shortcomings, and the chasm that often exists between what you practice and what you preach.

Whether running my business or writing a book about running my business, I am often reminded (sometimes by myself, sometimes by others) of my own inadequacies. But so what? The point has never been achieving perfection but the striving toward it, the commitment to improve daily, whether it be in one's business or in one's life.

This is the message that not only I have tried to convey but is reflective of the teachings and philosophy of many of my own personal heroes—Churchill, John and Bobby Kennedy, Sargent Shriver, Jack Kramer, to name a few. It is the message of excellence—as in excelling—of always trying to top yourself. And that one man, daring greatly in a noble cause, can make a difference. This, to me, has always been the beauty of the game of sport—that desire to excel, improve, and move up to the next level of competition. Progress may not always be smooth and easy but it is rare to meet the athlete who does not think he can play better or believes that he is only a short moment away from having his entire game fall into place.

I hope I have also conveyed the message that the "thrill of victory" is not just in winning but in *competing*—against others, against yourself. I can think of no better way to end this book than with the following quotation from Teddy Roosevelt, which expresses this sentiment so well as it sits, framed, on my desk in Washington:

> It is not the critic who counts; not the man who points out how the strong man stumbled, or where the doer of deeds could have done them better. The credit belongs to the man who is actually in the arena, whose face is marred by dust and sweat and blood; who strives valiantly; who errs and comes up short again and again; who knows the great enthusiasms, the great devotions; who spends himself in a worthy cause; who, at the best, knows in the end the triumph of high achievement and who, at the worst, if he fails, at least fails while daring greatly, so that his place shall never be with those timid souls who know neither victory nor defeat.

Serving clients in the right way provides a thrilling opportunity to make a positive difference every day in the lives of people. What could be more rewarding, more satisfying?

Therefore, whatever field of endeavor you choose . . . *be a player in the arena.* Whatever you can do or dream you can do, begin *now.*

ABOUT THE AUTHOR

A graduate of Yale and the University of Virginia Law School, DONALD L. DELL worked as special assistant to Sargent Shriver and then as an advance man in the 1968 campaign of presidential candidate Robert F. Kennedy. During the early 1960s, Dell was among the world's leading tennis players, having been ranked in the top ten in the United States four times, and was the winning U.S. Davis Cup team captain in 1968 and 1969. He founded ProServ, Inc., in 1970 in a two-man office overlooking an alley in Washington, D.C. His company has now grown into one of the world's leading international sports management and marketing firms, representing 250 athletes in fifteen different sports. He is married and lives on a farm in Potomac, Maryland, with his wife and twin children.